Addison Wesley

MW01250784

Science & Technology

TEACHER'S GUIDE

Grade 1

Authors
Lalie Harcourt
Ricki Wortzman

Sue Amos
Jane Deluzio
Ann Crysdale Gourlie
Dan Koenig
Jan Murphy
Ann Perron

Addison Wesley

Toronto

Program Developer: Doug Panasis, Resources.Too

Developmental Editor: Susan Petersiel Berg

Consultants: Dawn Hastings,
Tom Thompson School, Burlington,
Ontario

Donna Panasis,
St. Benedict's School, Markham,
Ontario

Margaret Ryall,
Avalon East School District,
St. John's, Newfoundland

Lionel Sandner,
Saanich School Board,
Saanich, British Columbia

Nancy Thomas,
Nahani Way Public School,
Mississauga, Ontario

Beverley Williams,
Coldbrook and District School,
Coldbrook, Nova Scotia

Editors: Susan Hughes
Naomi Pascoe
Shirley Tessier
Keltie Thomas

Researcher: Randi Solomon, B. Sc., B. Ed.

Acknowledgements
The publisher wishes to thank Ms. Maria Kemerer and her class at Regal Road Public School, Toronto, Ontario, and Mr. Farhan Hussain and his class at Wilkinson Public School, Toronto, Ontario, for their help with this book.

Photography
pages i, xvi, xvii, xxiii, 1, 12, 14, 15, 23, 33, 50, 54, 56, 57, 67, 72 (right), 76, 77, 78, 79, 80, 81, 89, 94, 100: Ian Crysler

pages iv (left), xii, xiii, xv (bottom left and right), 6, 10, 28, 34, 36: Ray Boudreau

page 72 (left): Tom McCrae

pages iv (right), v, xviii (bottom): Gilbert Duclos

Illustration
pages xxii – xxiii, AM 5, Energy LM 1, Energy LM 4: Vesna Krstanovich

pages 1, 30: Dorothy Siemens

pages 4, 6, 7, 9, 11, 28, 31, 50, 51, 52, 58, 73, 74, 75, 89, 94, 95, 96, 97, 102: June Bradford

pages 59, 67: Zena Denchik

page 99: Many Pens Design, Inc.

Line Masters: June Bradford

Copyright © 2000 Pearson Education Canada Inc., Toronto, Ontario

All rights reserved. This publication is protected by copyright, and permission should be obtained from the publisher prior to any prohibited reproduction, storage in a retrieval system, or transmission in any form or by any means, electronic, mechanical, photocopying, recording, or likewise. For information regarding permission, write to the Permissions Department.

Reproduction of the line masters for the use of one classroom is permitted.

The information and activities presented in this book have been carefully edited and reviewed. However, the publisher shall not be liable for any damages resulting, in whole or part, from the reader's use of this material.

0-13-027900-5

This book contains recycled product and is acid free.

Printed and bound in Canada.

2 3 4 5 — BBM — 04 03 02 01

Addison
Wesley

Table of Contents

Fostering Scientific Knowledge in Young Children

Young children have already learned a great deal about their environment when they enter school. As children play in the sandbox, build with blocks, follow the path of an ant, or splash in puddles, they make discoveries. Their natural curiosity and sense of wonder lead them to observe, compare, and predict. Typically their curiosity leads them naturally to test their ideas, then draw conclusions about their world and how things work. They already have the skills that are the building blocks of scientific literacy and knowledge.

The vision that guides *Addison Wesley Science & Technology Grades 1 and 2* is founded on a belief that all children can develop into scientifically literate adults. Building on their inherent sense of wonder, children can be encouraged to:

- develop an understanding of the relationships between science and technology and their own world, seeing connections between science and its social and environmental context

- develop the skills required for scientific and technological inquiry as they freely explore materials, design solutions to problems, and test out ideas

- understand the concepts of scientific knowledge as they pose questions and seek answers

and

- demonstrate a respect for scientific endeavour, a responsibility for the natural environment, and an interest in and positive disposition towards science that will serve them well in future years

The adults that surround young children, be they teachers or family, can:

- demonstrate that scientific and technological discovery is a valued part of education

- provide ongoing feedback to children in guided discussion, or during presentations and demonstrations

- enable children to take ownership and responsibility for their learning as they seek answers to their questions and then reflect and assess how well they met the challenges presented to them

and

- provide a range of activities for children: some that follow procedural steps, some that are open inquiry, and some that involve children investigating questions that are of personal interest

Program Components at Grades 1 & 2: An Overview

The *Addison Wesley Science & Technology for Grades 1 and 2* program includes:

Student Books

There are five *Student Books* for each of Grades 1 and 2. These books correspond to the strands of the curriculum.

Earth and Space Systems

Life Systems

Matter and Materials

Structures and Mechanisms

Energy and Control

Flip Chart Book

There is one *Flip Chart Book* for each grade level. These books include 18 double-page spreads from Student Books in an enlarged format to focus and facilitate learning experiences with the whole class.

Flip Chart Book

Teacher's Guide

There is one *Teacher's Guide* for each grade level that contains core lessons, curriculum-related activities, and assessment. Line Masters are included in the teacher's guides to serve as:

- support for materials for activities

- recording sheets for children

- tracking sheets for teachers

USING THE STUDENT BOOKS/FLIP CHART BOOKS

The *Student Books* in this program reflect the belief that a well-balanced science program must present:

- information about the concepts of science and technology that is relevant, engaging, and appropriate for young children

- a developmentally appropriate series of learning experiences

- a blend of different types of science activity; some that are open-ended, others that are guided

- many opportunities for children to relate science and technology to their environment as well as the world beyond

- the opportunity for children to share what they are learning with their families and to encourage their families to participate in the learning

Here are the different types of pages you will find in each Student Book.

Content pages provide a focal point to develop scientific and technological knowledge and reflect curriculum outcomes and expectations. These pages allow children to build on their experiences as they observe and relate the concepts of science and technology to what they already know. Each content spread ends with a question or statement that engages children in applying what they have observed and learned. *Note*: Many of these pages appear in enlarged format in the *Flip Chart Book* to facilitate whole class discussions and learning.

Many structures at the fair move. You can turn them on and off.

Which of these structures can be turned on and off?

Draw another ride that turns on and off.

Design Time

Build a structure for a model playground.

Think about what playground structure you will build.

Get what you need.

Build your structure.

Check it.

Finish it.

Tell about your structure.

Design Time pages engage children in developing their skills of design technology as they identify a problem, plan a design, build it, test it, and then communicate their findings.

Science & Technology

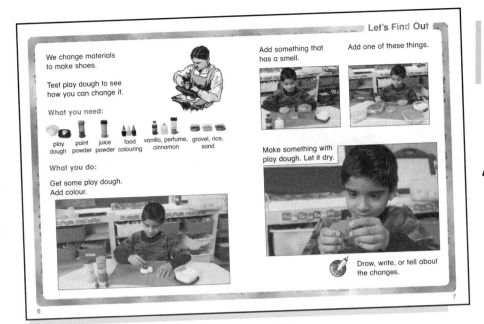

We change materials to make shoes.

Test play dough to see how you can change it.

What you need:

play dough | paint powder | juice powder | food colouring | vanilla, perfume, cinnamon | gravel, rice, sand

What you do:

Get some play dough.
Add colour.

Add something that has a smell.

Add one of these things.

Make something with play dough. Let it dry.

 Draw, write, or tell about the changes.

6

7

Let's Find Out pages enable children to pursue tasks on their own or in small groups as they follow an illustrated set of steps.

At Home pages engage the family in discovering ideas about science and technology together in the home environment.

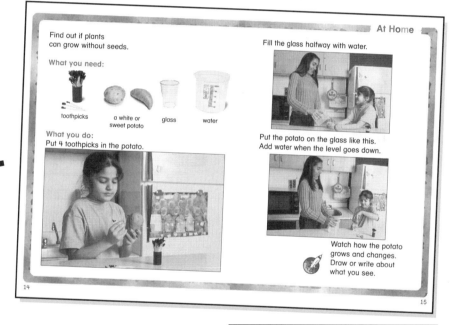

Find out if plants can grow without seeds.

What you need:

toothpicks | a white or sweet potato | glass | water

What you do:
Put 4 toothpicks in the potato.

Fill the glass halfway with water.

Put the potato on the glass like this.
Add water when the level goes down.

Watch how the potato grows and changes. Draw or write about what you see.

14

15

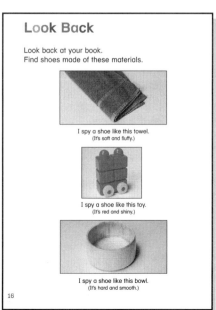

Look Back

Look back at your book.
Find shoes made of these materials.

I spy a shoe like this towel.
(It's soft and fluffy.)

I spy a shoe like this toy.
(It's red and shiny.)

I spy a shoe like this bowl.
(It's hard and smooth.)

16

A *Look Back* page invites children to revisit the Student Book and reflect on the unit as a whole.

A *Glossary* of key words on the inside back cover enables children to familiarize themselves with key vocabulary relevant to the science and technology unit.

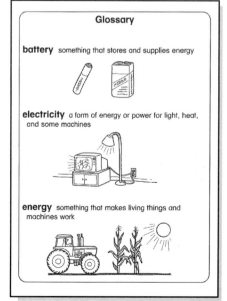

Glossary

battery something that stores and supplies energy

electricity a form of energy or power for light, heat, and some machines

energy something that makes living things and machines work

USING THE TEACHER'S GUIDE

The *Teacher's Guide* houses the complete science and technology program for each grade level. The five topics in each grade level are presented in an order that recognizes seasonal issues, the difficulty of concepts, and the overall flow of a typical school year.

Unit Overview

The first page of every unit describes the flow of the concepts and skills introduced, as well as issues particular to different topics. Any special considerations, including collecting necessary materials, are highlighted and discussed.

Changes All Around Me

UNIT OVERVIEW

In this unit children observe, compare, and investigate many of the natural cycles around them.

- The unit begins with **children** starting a Seasons Journal. They **record their observations** of the weather and the changes they see in the living things in their immediate environment. These records will give children the opportunity to see how the weather and the seasons affect the living things around them, including themselves. They observe and discuss how humans and animals adapt to different weather conditions.

- **Children also explore** the changes that take place during a day. They measure the temperature and chart the course of their shadows to develop an understanding of how heat and light from the sun changes over the course of a day.

- As **children develop an understanding** of the cycles and patterns in nature they see things as connected events rather than random ones. When children feel comfortable making predictions based on the patterns and the cycles around them it is an

how they can make thin shadows, thick shadows, and other shadows of varying shapes and sizes.

You might decide to have children make entries in their Seasons Journal on the first of every month, on the first day of each season, or at other regular intervals. The important thing is to set a schedule and keep to it. Children can only make comparisons and gain an appreciation of change over time if they have several different sets of data to work with.

Launch the Topic and Keep It Going

Each unit is launched through an activity. This activity starts the children thinking about the topic and engages them in communicating their ideas and questions about the unit topic, allowing you to access children's prior knowledge and perceptions about science concepts. The discussion you have at this point is typically charted and recorded. Children are encouraged to add to and revise the charts throughout the unit. This section ends with a suggestion to send home Family Letter A, which informs the family of the current science topic and suggests a variety of activities that can be done at home to support and enhance children's learning. Family Letter B is referred to in the *At Home* activity and can be sent home instead of the Student Book so that children and their families can complete the *At Home* activity together.

A LAUNCH THE TOPIC

Ask children to tell you the current date including the month. Then ask them to tell you the season. With their help list the other seasons and have them chant them in order several times.

Distribute a piece of paper to each child or pair of children and ask them to draw or write about one thing that they know for certain about one of the seasons. If they have difficulty, explain that they might record something about the weather, what they wear, what they do, what animals or plants look like, and so on. Have children who have chosen the same season sit together, and give all groups time to share their recordings. Then have each group think of some questions they would like to ask about the season they are discussing. List the questions on a chart titled: We Wonder about the Seasons.

KEEP IT GOING

Throughout the unit refer to the chart of We Wonder statements to see if any of them has been answered to the children's satisfaction. Record all of their responses or new thinking on a chart entitled: We Learned About the Seasons. Continue to record on the chart as you do each activity in this unit.

You might also wish to post chart paper and record new vocabulary as children encounter it during the unit.

As you begin this unit, send home Family Letter A. Encourage families to do some of the activities suggested to enhance children's learning about changes during the day and the seasons.

We Wonder

Why does it get cold in winter ?

When is it the hottest day ?

Do people everywhere have summer ?

How hot is the sun ?

Why are there 4 seasons ?

Unit Planner

The *Unit Planner*, in chart form, provides an at-a-glance view of all of the activities, materials, resources, and assessment options, to enable you to plan, teach, assess, and extend learning in each unit.

Activity Bank Activities

These activities meet the curriculum expectations and outcomes and are organized by the estimated amount of time they take to complete.

- *Take 5 Activities* can be repeated. Often it is through frequent and incidental exposure that children develop the skills and concepts introduced. These activities are suited for any spare five minutes—not just during a science lesson.

- *Take 30 Activities* last about one science class period and present the concepts of other core activities in another way or, in some instances, introduce concepts.

- *Take Time Activities* take longer than one class period and in most cases are intended to run throughout the unit and beyond. This is an opportunity for children to pursue their own questions and interests at a centre. Consider these ideas as a way to accommodate early finishers in meaningful activity.

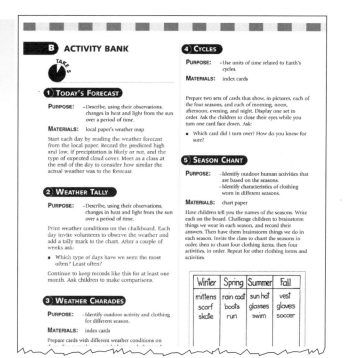

Cross-Curricular Overview

The activities on this page facilitate integrated learning by offering ways to link science and technology learning to other areas of the primary curriculum. The teaching suggestions follow the familiar lesson plan flow of the *Student Book/Flip Chart Book* activities in *Addison Wesley Science & Technology Grades 1 and 2*. The expectations of other subject areas such as Music, Art, Health and Physical Education, and Mathematics are listed. As well, one suggestion directly relates to one of the five Social Studies books in *Ginn Social Studies Grades 1 and 2*.

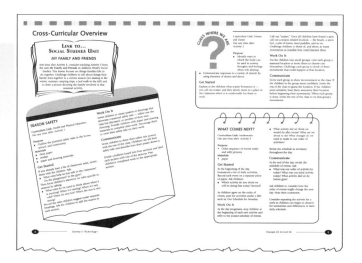

Student Book/Flip Chart Book Activities

Each of the lessons is linked directly to *Student Book* pages. All of these lessons follow the same lesson development and are supported with: purpose statements of expectations and outcomes, required materials, suggested duration, skill focus, questions related to sustainable development, and assessment opportunities. (*Note*: One class period is about 30 minutes.)

- *Get Started* outlines how to get the children engaged in thinking about the concepts and skills. Typically this part of a lesson is done with the whole class and may involve children in making a recording for a graph or chart, brainstorming and charting possibilities, going on a wonder walk, or participating in or observing a class demonstration

- *Work On It: Using Pages ___ and ___* focuses children's attention on material presented in their Student Books or Flip Chart Books. Questions and prompts are provided to initiate discussion. The purpose of the pages is to bring content to the children or to help to define the task, problems, and activities they will engage in next.

- *Work On It: Beyond the Page* presents an activity that is typically carried out in small groups or by individuals. Line Masters may be suggested to support the activity or for children to record observations and plans.

- *Communicate,* the last phase in a lesson, describes a consolidation discussion or activity that brings children back together, helps them reflect on what they have learned, and invites them to ask and pursue new questions they may have. As well, they often apply their new views and conceptions to other examples in the *Extension* section.

C STUDENT BOOK/FLIP CHART BOOK ACTIVITIES

Student Book pages 2–3

" There are four seasons in a year. Each season brings changes. "

PURPOSE:
- Compare the different characteristics of the four seasons.
- Use units of time related to Earth's cycles (for example, days, months, seasons).
- Use appropriate vocabulary in describing observations.
- Record relevant observations using drawings.

MATERIALS:
- mural paper
- drawing materials
- large sticky notes or paper the size of large index cards
- a copy of LM 1 for each child
- clipboards
- date stamp

TIME:
2 to 3 class periods

SKILL FOCUS:
observing, comparing, communicating

GET STARTED
On a large sheet of mural paper draw a very large circle. Divide it into quarters. Print Winter beside one quarter and say:
- Winter is one season. What are the other three seasons?

Record the correct responses to create the cycle of the seasons in order: winter, spring, summer, fall. Have the children chant the cycle of seasons several times and then suggest pictures that might tell us about each season.

After some discussion, divide the class into small groups and assign each a season. Provide each child with drawing materials and large sticky notes or pieces of paper the size of large index cards. Ask children to draw something for their group's season. When pictures are complete meet as a large group. Have children tell what they drew. Post their pictures in the appropriate place on the chart.

WORK ON IT

USING PAGES 2 AND 3
Encourage children to describe each scene in the book. Print the names of the seasons across a piece of chart paper. Ask the children to describe the tree in winter, and the other seasons, and record their descriptions. Repeat, asking about the children's activities, the people's clothing, and the type of weather.

BEYOND THE PAGE
Ask children to compare the pictures to the present season. Take the children outdoors to begin their Seasons Journal. Children should have a copy of LM 1, a pencil, and a clipboard or other hard surface. Explain that this is the first of many pages in their Seasons Journal.

Challenge them to make a drawing to show what the weather is like and include

anything they see, especially plants, grass, and any animals or birds. Explain that they will be observing the same area at different times in the year so it's important for them to record the date of their observations. (If possible, provide a date stamp.)

COMMUNICATE

Repeat these outdoor observations regularly, about once a month. Encourage children to look through their Seasons Journal to tell about the changes they have observed and recorded.

EXTENSION
Provide children with monthly calendars and invite them to record the daily weather.

ASSESSMENT OPPORTUNITY
The children's Seasons Journals will show work over a significant period of time, giving you an opportunity to see children's recording skills change. Track **portfolio** entries on AM 4.

At Home

At Home activities: The final double-page spread in each Student Book can be done at home or, if you prefer, in the classroom. Teaching notes to accommodate both approaches are provided.

Student Book pages 14–15

At Home

PURPOSE:

– Compare the characteristics of the seasons.

– Use units of time related to Earth's cycles.

– Identify outdoor human activities based on the seasons.

– Identify characteristics of clothing for different seasons and make appropriate decisions about clothing for different environmental conditions.

– Communicate with home.

MATERIALS:

GET STARTED

As a group, either look out the window or go outside. Invite children to describe any signs of the current season. Ask:

■ How can you tell that right now it is (fall)? What do you suppose would be different if it were winter right now? Spring? Summer?

Next, focus children's attention on the time of day. Ask:

■ How can you tell that it is now (morning)? What do you think would be different if it were night? Late afternoon?

WORK ON IT

USING PAGES 14 AND 15

As a class, choose one of the pictures on the page. Invite the children to give as

Send home the Student Book or Family Letter B and have children and their families complete the activity together. Alternatively, complete the activity in the classroom.

COMMUNICATE

Encourage children to bring to class family photos that were taken outdoors. Have children pass their photos around for others to see. You might add to the collection by including seasonal photographs cut from magazines or old calendars.

Once children have had a chance to explore, invite them to explain when they think the different photos were taken and to explain their reasons for choosing the season and time of day they do. You might direct children's attention to such aspects of the photos as the clothing people are

---

Look Back

The *Look Back* activity invites children to revisit their Student Book and reflect on the things they have observed and learned. As well, children can extend their self-reflections and articulate what they have learned on the Self-Assessment Line Master provided. *Note*: Some children will benefit from stating what they have learned to a scribe (teacher or aide) who can write for them.

Student Book page 16

Look Back

PURPOSE:

– Identify outdoor human activities that are based on the seasons.

– Identify characteristics of clothing worn in different seasons.

– Describe changes in the characteristics, behaviour, and location of living things that occur in seasonal cycles.

SKILL FOCUS:

observing

WORK ON IT

USING PAGE 16

Together, read page 16 in the Student Book and ensure that everyone understands the task. Have children complete the activity on the page. Looking back through the book will help remind children about appropriate dress and activities for specific weather conditions.

ANSWERS

There are eight situations inappropriate for the weather. They are:

■ person watering flowers
■ skater in a bathing suit
■ man barbequeing in short sleeves
■ man in bathing suit and boots, hat, scarf, and mittens

■ kid wearing snorkel gear
■ girl in taxi wearing a bathing suit
■ person in wheelchair wearing shorts
■ woman entering building wearing sandals

COMMUNICATE

Invite children to share what they found, and to talk about what they learned about daily and seasonal cycles.

ASSESSMENT OPPORTUNITY

Provide children with a copy of AM 5 for self-assessment. Discuss children's answers with them individually, and store completed Assessment Masters in children's portfolios.

 16 — Science & Technology 1

Demonstrate What You Know

The *Demonstrate What You Know* task is designed to further inform you of children's thinking. This activity is accompanied by a four-part rubric to establish the criteria for the work children do.

Demonstrate What You Know

PURPOSE:

– Assess children's learning.

MATERIALS:

• cards labelled with names of seasons
• large sheets of paper
• glue
• scissors
• LM 4 for each child

SKILL FOCUS:

observing, seriating, inferring

GET STARTED

Place cards with the names of the seasons on the chalkboard ledge in random order. Ask a volunteer to select one of the cards and post it on the chalkboard. Read it aloud together and then have volunteers select and post the appropriate cards in response to your directions to find what seasons come before and after. Discuss where to place the final card (at either end of the cycle) and why either choice is fine.

Read the cards in order several times. Have children close their eyes as you remove one card. Invite them to open their eyes and identify which season is missing and tell how they know.

ASSIGN THE TASK

Distribute LM 4. Ask children to describe what is happening in each picture. Explain

large sheets of paper, glue, and scissors. When children have completed the gluing they should label each picture with a seasonal word. They can refer to the cards posted earlier.

Have children show and explain their ordering. Ask:

■ How did you know that the picture showed fall? Summer and not spring?

Next, challenge children to draw people for each picture, either under the picture itself or on a separate sheet to be cut out and glued in place. Explain that the people must be dressed for the season and doing an activity that is appropriate for that time of year. Meet again for children to share their work when it is complete.

ASSESS THE TASK

The following will help you assess each child's learning about daily and seasonal

---

Creating an Environment for Scientific Learning

ENCOURAGING RESPONSIBLE ATTITUDES IN SCIENCE

Respect for the Environment

Many of the activities and trips in *Addison Wesley Science & Technology Grades 1 and 2* provide opportunities for children to develop a respect for living things and their environment. There are many ways you can support and model this positive attitude.

- Ensure the areas you visit are public property or that permission to visit has been obtained.

- Whenever possible observe nature in its natural habitat. Take only photographs, pictures, and lists back to the classroom. Step carefully and speak quietly.

- Collect samples in a way that won't harm plants, insects, or animals. Remember to provide children with disposable gloves.

- Provide a safe and healthy environment for any invertebrates or insects you borrow from nature. Collect some soil, twigs, leaves, and so on from their habitat and place them in the temporary home. Monitor their care while in the classroom to ensure their needs are being met.

- Release creatures and insects to an appropriate habitat as soon as possible.

- Return all collected samples such as rocks, soil, and shells to where they were found.

- Discuss ways to reduce, reuse, and recycle materials in the classroom. Establish thoughtful routines for conserving water and energy.

- Choose classroom pets and plants carefully and care for them in a knowledgeable, consistent, and respectful manner.

Safety

Safety is an important aspect of any program. In Science, there are many ways you can model and teach safe practices Many skills and practices related to safety have been identified in the overview of a unit or mentioned within a lesson. Here are some general guidelines.

- Obtain a copy of the safety policies and expectations set by your school board and the Ministry of Education and Training.

- At the start of an activity, discuss and highlight the do's and don'ts associated with any substances, tools, materials, or procedures.

- Be aware of and post all allergies.

- Ask children to check with you before tasting any substance. Establish a hygienic way of sampling edible foods.

- Show children how to smell substances safely by using their hand to waft the scent toward their noses.

- Check your classroom on a regular basis to ensure that equipment and materials are safe and that all safety precautions are being followed.

- Remind children not to touch their face or any part of their body while working with animals, plants, soil, or substances. Establish a hand-washing routine that follows each activity.

- Provide safety equipment such as gloves and goggles.

- Supervise children closely when they are using sharp implements, heat, or on an outdoor walk or activity.

- Encourage children to accept responsibility for their safety and that of others. Children should make you aware of any safety concerns.

- Help children keep their work space clean and organized.

Sustainable Development

Science involves the study of one's environment. One of a scientist's responsibilities to that environment is to study it and care for it in such a way that future generations can do the same. Even young children can understand that they have a role to play in sustaining the planet. Key concepts of sustainable development appropriate for this age include:

- energy use
- conservation of renewable and non-renewable resources
- preserving habitats

Through discussion, activities, and guided questioning, children can begin to become aware of and learn that they use a variety of energy sources, including gasoline, coal, and wood, in daily life. The more these resources are used, the more depleted they become. Humans are responsible for maintaining a healthy habitat, not just for future generations, but for all living things. As energy use increases, water, land, and air become polluted. Dirty lakes and larger landfills threaten wildlife and poison drinking water. Pollutants in the air have led to the thinning of the ozone layer, without which Earth's air temperature rises and all life is affected. Cutting down trees robs the soil of nutrients, decreases available vegetation for cleaning the air, and destroys the habitats of countless living creatures. Wind and water erode nourishing topsoil for farmers' crops, and overfishing has led to quotas and bans for commercial fishers.

National sustainable development programs include cleaning up the Great Lakes, reducing allowable emissions of greenhouse gases, promoting sustainable forestry practices, and implementing recycling programs in many cities across Canada.

In *Addison Wesley Science & Technology Grades 1 and 2*, questions and discussion topics related to sustainable development are included in Teacher's Guide lessons where relevant and appropriate.

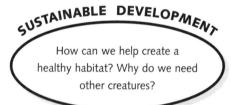

SUSTAINABLE DEVELOPMENT

How can we help create a healthy habitat? Why do we need other creatures?

ENCOURAGING ONGOING INQUIRY AND DISCOVERY

Science Centre

A *Science Centre* in the classroom encourages curiosity, hands-on involvement, sharing, questioning, experimenting, and discovery. You will find materials and activity suggestions for setting up a long-term science area or centre in the *Take Time* section of the Activity Bank activities section. As with any classroom centre, the management and organization of routines and materials facilitate the interest and success of the area. Here are some tips to consider.

- Organize and label materials so children can assume responsibility for their care and cleanup.

- Establish routines and guidelines about the use of space, noise, storage, and the safe handling of tools and materials.

- Establish an area to house general science materials such as magnifying lenses, measuring tools, safety equipment, and a range of materials for recording observations and discoveries.

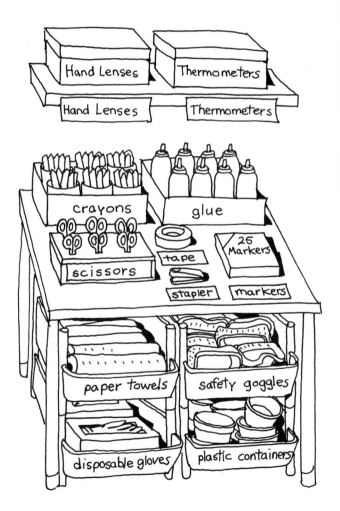

Wonder Board

Establishing a *Wonder Board* for each unit gives children the message that their knowledge, questioning, and learning are valued and respected. A *Wonder Board* can help you access children's prior knowledge while helping children connect new learning to existing knowledge.

A *Wonder Board* is featured in the Launch of each unit and as an inquiry tool in some activities. The *Wonder Board* is a simple chart posted with three headings: *We Know, We Wonder, We Learned.* In the first column, record what the children agree they know about a given topic. In the second, record the statements they could not agree upon, their questions, and the things they would like to find out. The third column provides a space for new information and answers. Children are encouraged to add to, edit, and revise the chart throughout the unit and possibly into the next.

Bulletin Boards

Bulletin Boards are a visual record of the work in progress. Many activities suggest displaying children's work and ideas on a bulletin board. Children can add to the display and refer to it as an information resource.

HELPING CHILDREN GATHER INFORMATION AND ANSWER QUESTIONS

Addison Wesley Science & Technology Grades 1 and 2 provides many inquiry activities and encourages children to plan investigations and find possible answers to their questions. By providing a range of resources and first-hand experiences, you facilitate the children's learning and their sense of accomplishment.

Direct Observation

For the young child, observing the real thing is the best source of information and discovery. Whenever possible, plan a field trip, take an observation walk, or explore samples of the objects under discussion.

People

People are a wonderful source of knowledge. Work with children to prepare questions before interviewing visitors.

Computers

Computers are one way children can access information. Some software programs and Web sites are featured in the *Planning Ahead* section of each Unit Planner. Consider checking your school library for suitable science software. For information on a wide variety of science topics, children might look at the following Web sites:

- Gander Academy's Theme-Related Resources on the World Wide Web:
  www.stemnet.nf.ca/CITE/themes.html
- Sciencenet: http://sciencenet.tpl.toronto.on.ca

You may find the Outreach Science Ontario Web site (www.biochem.uwo.ca/oso/strandchart.html) a useful teacher resource.

Books and Visual Reference Materials

As children develop their "Wonder" questions, begin to set up a science library of related pictures and books. Work with your school librarian to locate appropriate media materials such as films, videos, and software. You will find some suggestions in the *Planning Ahead* section of each Unit Planner.

HELPING CHILDREN DEVELOP SKILLS

The Inquiry Process

Science can be one of the most interesting and satisfying areas of study for young children. It builds on their natural curiosity about their world and the many things that are in it. It encourages them to become involved in activity, to talk, to try things out, to look around, and to ask questions. *Addison Wesley Science & Technology Grades 1 and 2* recognizes this natural learning style of the young child as it provides opportunities to develop their understanding of basic concepts and their skills of inquiry, design, and communication.

Let's Find Out activities in each Student Book follow a five-step inquiry process for science investigation.

STEP 1
Ask a Question
The class was asked to think about how their shadow will change during the day. Tasia and the other children shared their predictions.

STEP 2
Plan the Investigation
The class talked about where and when they would do their shadow investigations. They talked about ways to record their shadows so they could identify their own shadows and compare the changes that occurred.

STEP 3
Record Observations and Collect Data
Tasia worked with Marcus to make a tracing of her shadow at three different times in the day. She talked with Marcus after each tracing about what she noticed. At the end of the day the class talked about their observations. They did exactly the same thing for the next two days.

STEP 4
Make a Conclusion
The class worked together to share their observations and provide a reason for the patterns they had discovered. Tasia noticed that the higher the sun was in the sky, the shorter her shadow was!

STEP 5
Communicate the Findings
The teacher recorded their ideas on a chart and added it to the others that had been developed throughout the investigation. After asking children to summarize how their shadow changed throughout the day, he asked if they had other questions about shadows and how they change.

The Design Process

Design Time activities follow a five-step process for technology.

STEP 1

Identify a Task or Problem

The class brainstormed different structures they could make for a model playground. Marcia decided to design and build a playhouse.

STEP 2

Plan the Design

Marcia thought about the materials she needed and talked to her Grade 6 Buddy about her plans for putting it together. She wanted it to be the right size for the class model and sturdy enough to stand on its own.

STEP 3

Build the Design

Marcia had a problem getting her structure to stand up. She changed her plan and decided to use modelling clay as a base and for extra support .

STEP 4

Test the Design

Since Marcia had tested and revised as she worked, she is satisfied with how her structure looks and how stable it is.

STEP 5

Communicate

During the ribbon-cutting ceremony for the model playground, Marcia talked about the problems she had and showed how sturdy the playhouse is.

The Process Skills of science are embedded within the activities to help children gather, organize, communicate, and reflect on information. The following process skills have been incorporated into *Addison Wesley Science & Technology Grades 1 and 2.*

OBSERVING → using the senses to gather information

COMPARING → identifying similarities and differences

MEASURING → describing length, width, capacity, mass, volume, speed, and temperature

SERIATING → putting objects, events, or conditions in logical sequence

CLASSIFYING → sorting objects, events, or conditions according to predetermined criteria

COMMUNICATING → exchanging ideas, knowledge, and questions through speaking, writing, presenting, listening, viewing, and reading

INFERRING → making assumptions based on reasoning

HYPOTHESIZING → using observations and inferences to formulate possible explanations

PREDICTING → making decisions about what may happen based on first-hand experience or observations

EXPERIMENTING → planning and doing investigations to test predictions or hypotheses

CONTROLLING VARIABLES → manipulating conditions to determine the effect of those conditions on the results of an experiment

MAKING MODELS → representing objects by constructing replicas of them from different materials

INTERPRETING → using collected information to draw conclusions

Materials

Great care has been taken to suggest materials that are readily available, can be collected easily, or are inexpensive to purchase. By looking in the *Materials* list of the Unit Planner chart, you will see at a glance the materials needed for the unit. There are some suggestions on how to collect and organize these materials under the heading *Collecting Materials* on the opening page of each unit.

In addition to specific unit materials, there are some general science materials that you might like to have on hand to facilitate observation, safety, and recording.

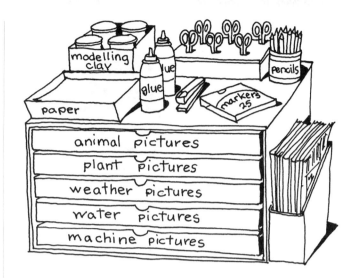

Observation Tools

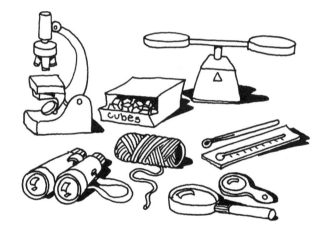

learning promotes movement, oral communication, and a rich supply of materials. Attention should be given to planning effective and efficient ways to organize and distribute materials. By stating clearly the expectations for movement, noise level, and handling of materials, you increase the children's level of independence and responsibility. As well as management tips included in the lessons, here are two general suggestions to keep in mind while planning an activity.

■ Place materials in a bin or shoebox and distribute them to groups or pairs. Keep general equipment in a central location so children can gather what they need and return it when they are finished.

Safety Equipment

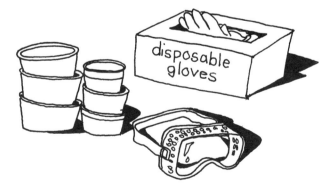

Recording Materials

Many activities in *Addison Wesley Science & Technology Grades 1 and 2* involve children in carrying out their own investigation or design plans. This approach to

- Keep materials in labelled bins. Provide each group, pair, or individual with a storage container such as a shoe box or large plastic bag, and invite each to select materials from the bins and carry them back to a work area.

Grouping

All lessons begin as a **whole group** so children can share prior knowledge or a common experience. Depending on the activity, children will either continue **on their own**, in a **small group,** or with a **partner**. Children come together as a **whole group** at the end of a lesson to share the procedures and communicate results of their work.

Communicating Scientific Learning

Communication is integral to science learning and can take many forms. Each activity in *Addison Wesley Science & Technology Grades 1 and 2* is rich with opportunities for discussion. Questions are provided both in the Student Books and Teacher's Guides to help you focus and orchestrate the sharing of ideas. You have likely observed that some children are more comfortable with one form of communicating than another. For example, the shy child or the child for whom English is a second language may like to write or draw rather than make an oral presentation, and the beginning writer may prefer to demonstrate ideas using different props. When children are exposed to a range of methods for communicating their learning, they are likely to begin by selecting ones that they feel comfortable and confident using. As they see the choices their peers make, they typically begin to try out other methods. The key to successful science learning is a commitment to ensuring that communication is integral to activity. Posting children's recordings and

displaying their models and constructions communicates to all who enter your classroom that science is an integral part of your program.

People	Animals	Plants
• they eat food	• there are lots of kinds	• they need water
• boys and girls	• some can fly	• flowers are pretty
• different colours of eyes	• some have fur	• trees give shade

By keeping notes of the comments, observations, questions, and ideas that children offer during class discussions, you model how print and sketches can capture the flow of ideas. You also send a clear message that you value children's input. Try to keep these recordings posted so that

- children can refer to them for appropriate vocabulary and spelling for their personal recordings

- you can connect future learning to past discussions

- it is possible to communicate children's discoveries and observations to an extended audience of classroom visitors

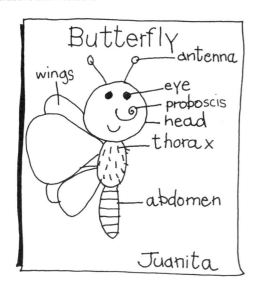

Graphs and *charts* are an effective way to communicate individuals' responses to specific questions. The act of interpreting a graph also engages children in posing questions, analyzing information, and then making summary statements.

Children's *writing* or *drawings* about what they have observed or what they have learned enables them to clarify their ideas and their thinking. When *recording* becomes an integral part of science activity, children come to feel more comfortable expressing themselves on paper and understand *recording* as an integral part of what scientists do.

Presenting *models* or participating in a *demonstration* are effective ways to communicate thinking and learning. As children explain their plans for the product and how they went about constructing it, they express their thinking and focus on the stated task, their plans, the procedure they followed, and the problems they encountered and solved along the way.

What did you wear on your hands today?						
Mittens	Claire	GURJIT	Zabi	Ian		
Gloves	Dudne	Yama	Bruce			
Nothing	Gina					

Assessing and Evaluating Progress

Assessing and evaluating children's progress is critical to planning an appropriate program that engages children and further develops their:

- understanding of basic concepts
- design and inquiry skills
- communication skills
- understanding of how science and technology relates to the world

Assessment is the actual gathering of information about the knowledge, skills, attitudes, interests, and needs of children. In *Addison Wesley Science & Technology Grades 1 and 2*, information about children's learning is gathered through:

- observations
- interviews
- self-assessments
- portfolios of children's work
- performance tasks

The information you gather then helps you to make an evaluation (assign a value or make a judgment) that reflects the quality of the work and thinking children have done over time in relation to the set expectations and criteria.

Observations

Observing children at work is a natural way for Primary teachers to gather information about young children's knowledge, skill development, and attitudes towards learning. Observations may be made informally as children participate in discussions, work on their own, or work in small groups. At other times you may choose a formal observation approach by actually planning and scheduling who you will observe and the purpose or focus of your observations.

A key to observing both informally and formally is good record-keeping. Of course, the method you use for recording observations in other subject areas may serve you well in Science. No matter what method you use, entries should be dated and the context noted. You may prefer to jot notes on file cards, in a notebook, on a gridded desk pad, or on a pad attached to a clipboard. Consider using self-stick notes so that you can easily transfer your notes. *Assessment Masters 1 and 2* are provided to help you with the task of recording and tracking your observations.

Interviews

Meeting with a child on a one-to-one basis can provide you with valuable information about the understandings a child has of the concepts introduced and the attitudes she or he has towards science inquiry. The meeting may be informal and take place as you visit a child at work. You might pose questions such as these to prompt reflection and sharing of thinking:

- Tell me about what you are doing right now. What did you do before?
- What problem are you trying to solve?
- What plans have you made?
- How are things going?
- Does what you are doing (observing, making, recording) remind you of anything we have done before?

Interviews can be formal in that you select a child and meet with her or him to get more information about a specific understanding, skill level, or attitudes. *Assessment Master 3* is provided to help you keep records of the interviews you conduct.

Portfolios

Keeping and filing samples of children's work over the course of the year enables you to see growth over time. Looking through a portfolio of work reminds you where a child began and provides you with evidence of the many changes that take place in a child's ability to communicate and a child's level of understanding over the course of a school year. Try to select pieces of significant work from each unit of study. You may want to involve children in selecting pieces of work for their portfolios or you may prefer to make the selections. The size and the format of the portfolio varies and usually depends on the materials and space available to you.

Assessment Master 4 is provided for you to attach to the outside of the folder to help you track entries and be aware of gaps between entries.

Self-Assessment

The questions you ask in class are constantly engaging children in reflecting on what they have done and what they are thinking. There is also a place for a formal self-assessment—one in which children take time to reflect and then record their thoughts about how and what they are doing as well as their attitudes towards learning. *Assessment Master 5* is provided and can be used at least once during each of the units. You may ask children to fill it out using words and/or drawings and in some cases you may need to record a child's dictated responses.

Performance Assessment

A performance assessment task provides you with more insight into a child's level of understanding. The task is related to the curriculum expectations and mirrors the type of activity typically taking place in the classroom.

One performance assessment task, the *Demonstrate What You Know* activity, is provided at the end of each unit. These tasks are designed to be easy to administer and involve children in creating a recording. They can be used with the entire class, or a smaller group if you so prefer. An accompanying four-part rubric will help you assess and evaluate children's work.

You might choose to identify an alternative activity to use as a performance task. *Assessment Master 6* is provided for you to create rubrics that would suit the performance tasks that you create.

Assessment Masters

ASSESSMENT MASTER 1 · · · · · · · · · · · GROUP OBSERVATION SHEET

ASSESSMENT MASTER 2 · · · · · · · · · · · INDIVIDUAL ASSESSMENT

ASSESSMENT MASTER 3 · · · · · · · · · · · INTERVIEW TRACKING SHEET

ASSESSMENT MASTER 4 · · · · · · · · · · · PORTFOLIO TRACKING SHEET

ASSESSMENT MASTER 5 · · · · · · · · · · · SELF-ASSESSMENT

ASSESSMENT MASTER 6 · · · · · · · · · · · RUBRIC MASTER

Note any observations that indicate :

- understanding of basic concepts
- inquiry and design skills
- communication of required knowledge
- relating of science and technology to each other and the world

Name:	Name:
Name:	Name:
Name:	Name:

Copyright © 2000 Pearson Education Canada Inc.

Name: _____   Date: _____

Science Unit: _____

Understanding basic concepts	
Inquiry and design skills	
Communication of required knowledge	
Relating of science and technology to each other and to the world outside the school	

  Copyright © 2000 Pearson Education Canada Inc.

Name	Date	Interview Notes	Next Steps

Copyright © 2000 Pearson Education Canada Inc.

My Portfolio

Name:_____

Title of Work   **Date Entered**

1 _____   _____

2 _____   _____

3 _____   _____

4 _____   _____

5 _____   _____

6 _____   _____

7 _____   _____

8 _____   _____

9 _____   _____

10 _____   _____

Copyright © 2000 Pearson Education Canada Inc.

Name: _____   Date: _____

This is what I did in science.

This is what I learned.

This is my new question.

Copyright © 2000 Pearson Education Canada Inc.

Unit: _____

Performance Task	
Rubric	**Criteria**
Level 4	
Level 3	
Level 2	
Level I	

Child's Name: _____   Date: _____

Level: _____

Comments: _____

_____

_____

_____

Copyright © 2000 Pearson Education Canada Inc.

Science & Technology
Changes All Around Me

Changes All Around Me

UNIT OVERVIEW

In this unit children observe, compare, and investigate many of the natural cycles around them.

- The unit begins with **children** starting a Seasons Journal. They **record their observations** of the weather and the changes they see in the living things in their immediate environment. These records will give children the opportunity to see how the weather and the seasons affect the living things around them, including themselves. They observe and discuss how humans and animals adapt to different weather conditions.

- **Children also explore** the changes that take place during a day. They measure the temperature and chart the course of their shadows to develop an understanding of how heat and light from the sun changes over the course of a day.

- As **children develop an understanding** of the cycles and patterns in nature they see things as connected events rather than random ones. When children feel comfortable making predictions based on the patterns and the cycles around them it is an indication that they expect things to make sense and that they have an understanding of how events and behaviours are related.

CONCEPT DEVELOPMENT AND OTHER ISSUES

This unit is best started early in the year so that children have the opportunity to observe changes around them over an extended period of time. Consider repeating many of the activities during different seasons to further develop the concept of change as a recurring and predictable process of events. Measuring temperature and charting the course of shadows are activities that should happen several times over the course of the year so that children understand that there is change over the course of a day and over the course of a year.

Children will likely have questions about shadows and why they move as they do. The higher the sun is in the sky, the shorter the shadow will be that the child sees.

After children complete the activities about shadows, they may be interested in the challenge of finding out how they can make thin shadows, thick shadows, and other shadows of varying shapes and sizes.

You might decide to have children make entries in their Seasons Journal on the first of every month, on the first day of each season, or at other regular intervals. The important thing is to set a schedule and keep to it. Children can only make comparisons and gain an appreciation of change over time if they have several different sets of data to work with.

COLLECTING MATERIALS

The nature of this unit is one of *observation, comparison,* and *prediction.* Other than a good *outdoor thermometer* there are no materials that require special collection or preparation.

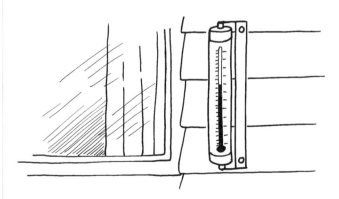

Unit Planner

ACTIVITY FOCUS ➡ CHILDREN:	TIME	MATERIALS
A **LAUNCH THE TOPIC ACTIVITY**		
state what they know about seasons; create questions for inquiry and investigation	1 class period	paper, chart paper
B **ACTIVITY BANK ACTIVITIES**		
❶ **Today's Forecast** — describe changes in heat and light from the sun over time	**Take 5**	local paper's weather map
❷ **Weather Tally** — describe changes in heat and light from the sun over time		
❸ **Weather Charades** — identify outdoor human activity and clothing based on seasons		index cards
❹ **Cycles** — use units of time related to Earth's cycles		index cards
❺ **Season Chant** — identify outdoor human activity and clothing based on seasons		chart paper
❻ **A Warm School** — identify features of houses that keep us sheltered and comfortable	**Take 30**	
❼ **Favourite Seasons** — compare characteristics of the four seasons		large sticky notes
❽ **If I Could Choose** — identify outdoor human activity and clothing based on seasons		
❾ **Observing Change** — describe changes in characteristics of living things on a daily basis		paper, drawing materials, date stamp, binoculars
❿ **Adopt a Tree** — describe changes in characteristics of living things over time	**Take Time**	paper, drawing materials, camera
⓫ **Season Collage** — identify outdoor human activity and clothing based on seasons		mural paper, print materials for cutting, scissors, glue
⓬ **A Day of Summer in Winter** — identify outdoor human activities based on seasons		
⓭ **Weather and Clothing Changes** — identify outdoor human activity and clothing based on seasons		chart paper
C **STUDENT BOOK/FLIP CHART BOOK ACTIVITIES**		
❶ **There are four seasons in a year. Each season brings changes.** — *pages 2-3* identify and describe the characteristics of the four seasons	1 class period plus	mural paper, drawing materials, sticky notes or index cards, clipboard, date stamp
❷ **Living things change during the seasons.** — *pages 4-5* observe how living things change during the seasons	1 to 2 class periods	chart paper
❸ **Weather changes during each season.** — *pages 6-7* identify how weather changes during the seasons	1 class period	chart paper, marker, materials for building such as found materials, craft materials, modelling clay
❹ **When seasons change, we do different things outside.** — *pages 8-9* identify outdoor seasonal activities	1 class period	drawing materials, paper
❺ **Weather changes during the day.** — *pages 10-11* identify how weather changes during the day	3 20-minute periods in one day	outdoor thermometer
❻ **Shadows change during the day.** — *pages 12-13* observe changes in light over time	3 20-minute periods in one day	chalk in different colours
❼ **At Home** — *pages 14-15* compare characteristics of the four seasons; use units of time related to the Earth's cycles	equivalent of 1 class period	
❽ **Look Back** — *page 16* reflect on and synthesize what they know	1 class period	
D **DEMONSTRATE WHAT YOU KNOW TASK**		
❶ describe and order seasonal pictures	1 class period plus	cards labelled with names of seasons, large sheets of paper, glue, scissors

ACTIVITY DESCRIPTION CHILDREN:	LINE MASTERS	ASSESSMENT
- write/draw what they know about seasons; create a 'Know/Wonder/Learned' chart	Family Letter Master A	interview
- read/record weather forecast from local paper		
- observe and chart weather over time		
- role-play weather conditions and appropriate clothing		
- predict season		
- chant names of seasonal clothing and activities		
- take a tour to see the school furnace		
- graph favourite seasons and other seasonal information		
- tell about a perfect day outdoors		
- observe and record changes viewed from a window		portfolio
- 'adopt' a tree and observe its changes over time		portfolio
- collaborate on a class seasons mural		
- plan a seasonal day out of season		
- discuss and graph clothing changes appropriate to weather		observation
- begin a Seasons Journal of observations about the seasons	LM 1	portfolio
- draw a filmstrip of their own changes during the seasons	LM 2	observation, portfolio
- make something to protect themselves from the weather		observation
- draw a machine or facility that makes seasonal activities possible any time		observation
- measure and record temperature throughout the day	LM 3	observation
- observe and record the movement of their shadow throughout the day		observation, interview
- identify the season and time of day in family photos	Family Letter Master B	
- identify who is not dressed for winter		
- describe characteristics of the seasons	LM 4	rubric

PLANNING AHEAD

TEACHER RESOURCES

Richards, Roy. An Early Start to Science. London: Macdonald Educational, 1987.

Wasserman, Selma and Ivany, George. Who's Afraid of Spiders? New York: Harper & Row, 1988.

BOOKS FOR CHILDREN

Helldorfer, M.C. Gather Up, Gather In. New York: Viking, 1994.

Hopkins, Lee Bennet. Weather: Poems for All Seasons. New York: Harper Trophy, 1994.

Lewis, Kim. First Snow. Cambridge, MA: Candlewick, 1996.

Morgan, Allen. Sadie and the Snowman. Toronto: Kids Can Press, 1985.

Pearson, Susan. My Favourite Time of Year. New York: Harper & Row, 1988.

WEB SITES

The Green Lane Home Page: www.ec.gc.ca/envhome.html

Snowtastic Snow: http://tqjunior.advanced.org/3876

BrainPOP (Seasons): www.brainpop.com/seasons

CD-ROMS

Sammy's Science House Ages 3-6 by Edmark Corporation.Win/Mac

Everything Weather by Sunburst Communications.Win/Mac

A Tree Through the Seasons by Goodmedia/Discis.Win/Mac

VIDEOS

Autumn
  B.C. Learning Connection Inc.

Bringing the Rain to Kapiti Plain
  B.C. Learning Connection Inc.

The Marsh: Nature's Nursery
  B.C Learning Commission Inc.

Cross-Curricular Overview

LINK TO...
SOCIAL STUDIES UNIT
MY FAMILY AND FRIENDS

Any time after Activity 4, consider teaching Activity 3 from the unit **My Family and Friends** in Ginn Social Studies. This lesson focuses on things families like to do together. Challenge children to tell about things their family does together in a certain season (ice skating in the winter, summer camping trips, a leaf walk in the fall) and to draw a picture showing the family involved in that seasonal activity.

SEASON SAFETY

Curriculum Link: *Health and Physical Education*
Use any time after: Activity 1

Purpose
- Outline the potential safety risks in the home, school, and community.

Materials
- chart paper
- marker
- paper and drawing materials

Get Started
If you already have a list of classroom rules, revisit them with the children. Ask:
- What rules help us stay safe in the classroom? On the playground? In the gym?

Then focus children's attention on rules specific to seasons by asking:
- What rules do we need to think about when it is snowing? When it's raining? When it's very cold? When it's very hot? When the sun is very strong?

Record the rules children suggest under separate headings. Ask the children to add the season to each section.

Work On It
Invite children to create posters or drawings that showcase a seasonal safety rule — either one the class has discussed, or another of their own choosing. Provide children with paper and drawing materials to complete their work. Encourage them to write their safety rule on their work.

Communicate
Invite children to share their safety rule posters with the rest of the class. Children can tell their safety rule and describe how their poster shows it.

Divide a bulletin board into four sections and label each section with one of the seasons. Post children's completed work in the appropriate section.

GUESS WHERE WE ARE

Curriculum Link: *Drama and Dance*
Use any time after: Activity 2

Purpose
- Identify ways in which the body can be used to convey thoughts and feelings when role playing.
- Communicate responses to a variety of stimuli by using elements of drama and dance.

Get Started
Explain to the children what scatter formation is — you call out scatter, and they slowly move to a place in the classroom where it is comfortable for them to work.

Call out "scatter." Once all children have found a spot, call out a season-related location — the beach, a snow fort, a pile of leaves, mud puddles, and so on. Challenge children to think of, and show, as many movements as possible that could happen there.

Work On It
Put the children into small groups. Give each group a seasonal location or invite them to choose one themselves. Challenge each group to think of three movements that could happen at that location.

Communicate
Invite each group to show its movement to the class. If the children in the group seem confident, invite the rest of the class to guess the location. If the children seem tentative, have them announce their location before beginning their movements. When each group is done, invite the rest of the class to try that group's movements.

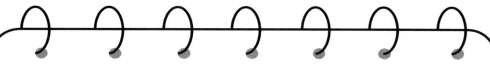

WHAT COMES NEXT?

Curriculum Link: *Mathematics*
Use any time after: Activity 5

Purpose
- Order sequence of events orally and with pictures.

Materials
- paper

Get Started
At the beginning of the day, brainstorm a list of daily activities. Record each event on a separate piece of paper. Ask children:
- Which activity do you think we will be doing first today? Second?

As children agree on the order of events, post the activities under a title such as, Our Schedule for Monday.

Work On It
As the day progresses, stop children at the beginning of each new activity and refer to the posted schedule of events.

- What activity did we think we would do after recess? What are we about to do? What changes do we need to make to our order of activities?

Revise the schedule as necessary throughout the day.

Communicate
At the end of the day, revisit the schedule of events. Ask:
- What was our order of activity for today? What was our third activity today? What activity did we do before gym?

Ask children to consider how the order of events might change the next day. Note their comments.

Consider repeating the activity for a week so children can begin to observe the similarities and differences in their daily schedule.

A LAUNCH THE TOPIC

Ask children to tell you the current date including the month. Then ask them to tell you the season. With their help list the other seasons and have them chant them in order several times.

Distribute a piece of paper to each child or pair of children and ask them to draw or write about one thing that they know for certain about one of the seasons. If they have difficulty, explain that they might record something about the weather, what they wear, what they do, what animals or plants look like, and so on. Have children who have chosen the same season sit together, and give all groups time to share their recordings. Then have each group think of some questions they would like to ask about the season they are discussing. List the questions on a chart titled: We Wonder about the Seasons.

KEEP IT GOING

Throughout the unit refer to the chart of We Wonder statements to see if any of them has been answered to the children's satisfaction. Record all of their responses or new thinking on a chart entitled: We Learned About the Seasons. Continue to record on the chart as you do each activity in this unit.

You might also wish to post chart paper and record new vocabulary as children encounter it during the unit.

As you begin this unit, send home Family Letter A. Encourage families to do some of the activities suggested to enhance children's learning about changes during the day and the seasons.

> ## We Wonder
>
> Why does it get cold in winter ?
> When is it the hottest day ?
> Do people everywhere have summer ?
> How hot is the sun ?
> Why are there 4 seasons ?

B ACTIVITY BANK

1 TODAY'S FORECAST

PURPOSE: –Describe, using their observations, changes in heat and light from the sun over a period of time.

MATERIALS: local paper's weather map

Start each day by reading the weather forecast from the local paper. Record the predicted high and low, if precipitation is likely or not, and the type of expected cloud cover. Meet as a class at the end of the day to consider how similar the actual weather was to the forecast.

2 WEATHER TALLY

PURPOSE: –Describe, using their observations, changes in heat and light from the sun over a period of time.

Print weather conditions on the chalkboard. Each day invite volunteers to observe the weather and add a tally mark to the chart. After a couple of weeks ask:

■ Which type of days have we seen the most often? Least often?

Continue to keep records like this for at least one month. Ask children to make comparisons.

3 WEATHER CHARADES

PURPOSE: –Identify outdoor activity and clothing for different season.

MATERIALS: index cards

Prepare cards with different weather conditions on them. For example, you might have cards that read: raining, snow falling, very hot, freezing cold. Have a volunteer choose a card and act out that type of weather. Ask:

■ What might you wear on such a day? What might you do?

sun	☀	cloud	☁
rain	🌧	snow	❄

4 CYCLES

PURPOSE: –Use units of time related to Earth's cycles.

MATERIALS: index cards

Prepare two sets of cards that show, in pictures, each of the four seasons, and each of morning, noon, afternoon, evening, and night. Display one set in order. Ask the children to close their eyes while you turn one card face down. Ask:

■ Which card did I turn over? How do you know for sure?

5 SEASON CHANT

PURPOSE: –Identify outdoor human activities that are based on the seasons.
–Identify characteristics of clothing worn in different seasons.

MATERIALS: chart paper

Have children tell you the names of the seasons. Write each on the board. Challenge children to brainstorm things we wear in each season, and record their answers. Then have them brainstorm things we do in each season. Invite the class to chant the seasons in order, then to chant four clothing items, then four activities, in order. Repeat for other clothing items and activities.

Winter	Spring	Summer	Fall
mittens	rain coat	sun hat	vest
scarf	boots	glasses	gloves
skate	run	swim	soccer

6) A WARM SCHOOL

PURPOSE: —Identify features of houses that help keep us sheltered and comfortable throughout daily and seasonal cycles.

Arrange with the school custodian to take the children to see the school furnace. Encourage the children to prepare questions to ask the custodian about how the furnace heats the school. On this tour also ask the custodian to tell other ways that the building stays warm in the winter.

SUSTAINABLE DEVELOPMENT

How can we use less heat and still stay warm? Why is this good?

7) FAVOURITE SEASONS

PURPOSE: —Compare the different characteristics of the four seasons.

MATERIALS: large sticky notes

Have each child print his or her name on a large sticky note. Print: Winter, Spring, Summer, Fall above the ledge of the chalkboard. Ask:

- Which is your favourite season?

In turn, they can place their name cards above the words to create a graph.

Interpret the graph by asking:

- What can you tell about our class from this graph?

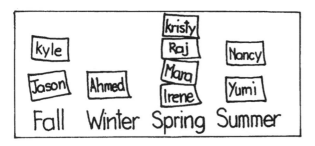

Encourage children to explain why they chose the season they did. You can create other class graphs related to weather and seasons. Here are some ideas:

- What is your favourite winter activity?
- What is your favourite summer activity?
- Which do you like better — hot days or cold days?
- How many sunny days were there this month?

8) IF I COULD CHOOSE

PURPOSE: —Identify outdoor activities based on seasons.

Encourage children to tell about what they think a perfect day outdoors would be. Ask:

- What would the weather be like? What would you do? What would you wear?

Children might make up a play, draw a picture, or write a story to tell about their choices and decisions.

9) OBSERVING CHANGES

PURPOSE: —Describe changes in the characteristics of living things that occur on a daily basis.

MATERIALS: paper
drawing materials
date stamp
binoculars

Set up a place at the window where children can look out to observe changes. Place paper, drawing materials, and a date stamp nearby to encourage children to record their observations. You might even consider making a pair of binoculars available for children to use. Post the children's observations and encourage children to think about how things have changed and what changes they predict will happen.

10) ADOPT A TREE

PURPOSE: —Describe changes in the characteristics, behaviour, and location of living things that occur in seasonal cycles.

MATERIALS: paper
drawing materials
camera (optional)

As a class adopt a nearby tree. Visit it regularly looking for changes each time. You might have children draw pictures on each visit or you might take photographs. Record children's observations in print and after each visit ask:

- How has the tree changed? What do you think it will look like on our next visit?

11) SEASON COLLAGE

PURPOSE: –Identify outdoor human activities that are based on the seasons.
–Identify characteristics of clothing worn in different seasons.

MATERIALS: mural paper
print materials for cutting
scissors
glue

Children can work as a class to create a collage of the seasons. Divide a large piece of mural paper into four sections. Label each one with a season. Provide magazines, brochures, old calendars, and travel catalogues and encourage children to look through them and cut out pictures related to the seasons. Children can then sort and glue the pictures onto the appropriate section of the mural paper. Post the mural paper and encourage children to continue to look for pictures.

12) A DAY OF SUMMER IN WINTER

PURPOSE: –Identify outdoor human activities that are based on the seasons.
–Identify characteristics of clothing worn in different seasons.

As a class work together to plan a day of summer in winter. Discuss what you should bring to school to wear, the activities you might do, and the food you could eat. Decorate the classroom and have a good time thinking about another season — out of season!

13) WEATHER AND CLOTHING CHANGES

PURPOSE: –Identify characteristics of clothing worn in different seasons.

MATERIALS: chart paper

On days when the weather changes, focus on the clothing that children wear. For example, on the first day of snow or on a day of rain, have the children show what they wore to school. On very hot days talk about the type of clothing that helps keep you cool. Use the children's responses to create graphs of their clothing. Here are some questions that can lead to graphing responses:

- It snowed today. What did you wear on your hands?

- Did you wear boots today?

- What did you wear: a raincoat, a snowsuit, or a spring jacket?

- Did you wear a hat today?

What did you wear on your hands?

mittens	gloves	nothing

Student Book pages 2–3

PURPOSE:

- Compare the different characteristics of the four seasons.
- Use units of time related to Earth's cycles (for example, days, months, seasons).
- Use appropriate vocabulary in describing observations.
- Record relevant observations using drawings.

MATERIALS:

- mural paper
- drawing materials
- large sticky notes or paper the size of large index cards
- a copy of LM 1 for each child
- clipboards
- date stamp

TIME:

2 to 3 class periods

SKILL FOCUS:

observing, comparing, communicating

" There are four seasons in a year. Each season brings changes. "

GET STARTED

On a large sheet of mural paper draw a very large circle. Divide it into quarters. Print Winter beside one quarter and say:

- Winter is one season. What are the other three seasons?

Record the correct responses to create the cycle of the seasons in order: winter, spring, summer, fall. Have the children chant the cycle of seasons several times and then suggest pictures that might tell us about each season.

After some discussion, divide the class into small groups and assign each a season. Provide each child with drawing materials and large sticky notes or pieces of paper the size of large index cards. Ask children to draw something for their group's season. When pictures are complete meet as a large group. Have children tell what they drew. Post their pictures in the appropriate place on the chart.

WORK ON IT

USING PAGES 2 AND 3

Encourage children to describe each scene in the book. Print the names of the seasons across a piece of chart paper. Ask the children to describe the tree in winter, and the other seasons, and record their descriptions. Repeat, asking about the children's activities, the people's clothing, and the type of weather.

BEYOND THE PAGE

Ask children to compare the pictures to the present season. Take the children outdoors to begin their Seasons Journal. Children should have a copy of LM 1, a pencil, and a clipboard or other hard surface. Explain that this is the first of many pages in their Seasons Journal.

Challenge them to make a drawing to show what the weather is like and include

anything they see, especially plants, grass, and any animals or birds. Explain that they will be observing the same area at different times in the year so it's important for them to record the date of their observations. (If possible, provide a date stamp.)

COMMUNICATE

Repeat these outdoor observations regularly, about once a month. Encourage children to look through their Seasons Journal to tell about the changes they have observed and recorded.

EXTENSION

Provide children with monthly calendars and invite them to record the daily weather.

ASSESSMENT OPPORTUNITY

The children's Seasons Journals will show work over a significant period of time, giving you an opportunity to see children's recording skills change. Track **portfolio** entries on AM 4.

"Living things change during each season."

PURPOSE:

- Describe changes in the characteristics, behaviour, and location of living things that occur in seasonal cycles.
- Use appropriate vocabulary in describing observations.
- Identify characteristics of clothing worn in different seasons and make appropriate decisions about clothing for different environmental conditions.

MATERIALS:

- copies of LM 2 for each child
- chart paper
- empty paper towel rolls or shoe boxes

TIME:

1 to 2 class periods

SKILL FOCUS:

observing, comparing, seriating, communicating

GET STARTED

Take the children outdoors to observe living things during the present season. Encourage them to look closely at trees and other plants and to be on the lookout for signs of animals, birds, and insects. Talk about the traces birds and animals leave, such as feathers, tracks, and parts of nuts, and encourage children to look for traces.

If possible, in the spring or fall, document children's observations by taking photographs of the living things children see. Invite children to create captions for the developed photos. Repeat this activity on a regular basis.

WORK ON IT

USING PAGES 4 AND 5

Encourage children to take a careful look at the movie of the maple tree in the student book. Discuss how the maple tree changes during the year. Then ask the children to think of a caption for each frame. Record their ideas on chart paper. Invite them to think of a title for the movie.

Then have children describe each frame of the movie of the bear and suggest captions. Discuss how the activity of the bear changes in each season.

Encourage children to think of how they change during the seasons. Ask:

- How does your clothing change? What activities do you do in each season? If someone were to take a photograph of you outside in winter, what might it look like? In summer?

BEYOND THE PAGE

Provide children with copies of LM 2, a template for creating a movie of themselves during the seasons. Explain that they need to do a minimum of four frames, but that they can do more by attaching together several copies of the line master.

Demonstrate to encourage children to roll their 'film' onto empty paper towel rolls or dowels to create a movie, or weave the 'film' through a shoe box. Invite children to add text to their drawings.

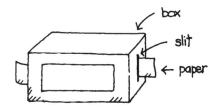

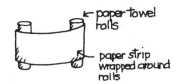

COMMUNICATE

Have children share their movies and explain how they are affected by seasons during one year.

EXTENSION

Children might also create a movie to show how they change from early morning to night. They can show how they might change their clothes and their activities.

ASSESSMENT OPPORTUNITY

Reflect on how children participate during discussion. Are they able to describe changes related to the seasons? Encourage children to describe the conditions of the present season. **Observations** can be recorded on AM 1 or AM 3. The movie is a good **portfolio** entry.

SUSTAINABLE DEVELOPMENT

What can we do to help trees grow? Why is it important to have healthy trees?

" Weather changes during each season. "

PURPOSE:

— Identify characteristics of clothing worn in different seasons and make appropriate decisions about clothing for different environmental conditions.

— Design and construct models of structures that would provide protection from local weather conditions.

— Identify features of houses that help keep us sheltered and comfortable daily and seasonally.

— Identify needs or problems arising from observable events and explore possible solutions.

— Communicate procedures and results of investigations.

MATERIALS:

• chart paper and marker materials such as egg cartons, paper, wires, pipe cleaners, fabric swatches, plastic bags, foil, craft sticks, modelling clay
• other materials for model-making as requested by children
• scissors
• glue

TIME:

1 class period

SKILL FOCUS:

making models, communicating

GET STARTED

Engage children in thinking about how they protect themselves from different weather conditions. Begin by asking them to describe the weather and what they wore to school. Record children's responses on chart paper. Ask:

■ Did you wear anything special to protect yourself? To make yourself more comfortable? When do you wear boots? What do you wear when it rains? What do you wear when it's sunny? What do you wear to go swimming? When do you wear a heavy coat? A light coat?

Encourage children to think about appropriate shelters for certain weather conditions by asking:

■ How do our home protect us from rain? Cold? Heat? The sun? What other shelters would help to protect you from weather?

WORK ON IT

USING PAGES 6 AND 7

Together, read the directions on the page. Ask:

■ What could you make to protect yourself from the weather? How could you keep yourself dry? Warm? Cool?

Have children choose a kind of weather, think about the problems presented, and then think about what they could make to protect themselves from that weather. Explain that they are going to make that item. Show them the available materials and invite them to choose what they need and to request any other items they need. Some children might like to select a toy figure to represent themselves. Provide them with plenty of time to make their model.

Visit children at work to see how they approach the task of designing and constructing their models.

BEYOND THE PAGE

Invite children to share their models. Ask:

■ What type of weather are you trying to protect yourself from? What did you make? What materials did you use? Did you have any problems? How did you solve them? What might you do differently next time?

COMMUNICATE

Encourage children to show how they tested their model. Display their finished models in the classroom. Children may wish to create another model of an item that protects them from a different kind of weather. Invite children to show and explain their work to you.

EXTENSION

Take a walk through the school playground or the neighbourhood to see if there are any places where people can take shelter from inclement weather. Encourage children to look for bus shelters, covered play areas, and so on.

ASSESSMENT OPPORTUNITY

This lesson engages children in identifying a problem and then looking for solutions. AM 1, AM 2, and AM 3 are provided for you to note **observations** and responses. Are children able to state the problems facing people in different weather conditions? What type of solutions do they come up with? Are children able to communicate their solutions clearly?

PURPOSE:

– Identify outdoor human activities that are based on the seasons and examine some of the solutions humans have found to make it possible to engage in these activities out of season.

MATERIALS:

• drawing materials
• paper

TIME:

1 class period

SKILL FOCUS:

classifying, interpreting, inferring

" **When seasons change, we do different things outside.** "

GET STARTED

Invite children to draw one of their favourite outdoor activities. Meet to discuss their drawings. As children present their pictures ask them to tell when during the year they do the activity. Sort the pictures together into two groups: activities we can do anytime and activities we only do during certain seasons. Challenge children to help sort the season-specific activities into the correct seasons. Post the pictures to create a graph.

Engage the children in thinking about the activities they have drawn. Ask:

■ Are there any activities that we can only do in (winter)? Why is it impossible to do at another time of year? Are there any activities you do at recess only in (winter)?

WORK ON IT

USING PAGES 8 AND 9

Invite volunteers to read the pages aloud. Have them pay attention to each situation as you ask:

■ Why can't you skate outdoors in the summer? What makes it possible to skate in the summer? Why can't you grow flowers outdoors in the winter? Where can you grow flowers in the winter? What have people done so that we can do these things in a different season?

BEYOND THE PAGE

Encourage children to work in small groups to think of other activities that could be on the page. Ask:

■ How are the pictures on this page alike? What other pictures could belong on this page?

List the situations that children suggest. Some interested children may offer to draw pictures of these suggestions. Display their pictures on a bulletin board with the heading In and Out of Season.

Encourage children to suggest activities that they would like to do in (summer). Ask what would make it possible for them to do these activities in summer. Then invite them to draw a design of a machine or facility that would make that possible. For example, children might draw a facility or machine that would allow them to toboggan in summer or to play baseball in winter.

COMMUNICATE

Invite children to share their designs with the rest of the class. Encourage them to describe their facility and its features. Post children's designs on a bulletin board so they can revisit their classmates' designs.

EXTENSION

Consider planning a field trip to an indoor facility such as a skating rink or swimming pool. Arrange to have employees explain to the children how the building is maintained—how ice is made or how water temperature is controlled. Children might also enjoy a trip to a greenhouse where they can find out how an environment conducive to growing things in all weather conditions is maintained.

ASSESSMENT OPPORTUNITY

Listen to how children participate in class discussions. Are they willing to offer ideas and suggestions? Do they pose questions? Do they understand the concepts? Can they explain how environments are controlled so that they can do activities out of season?

SUSTAINABLE DEVELOPMENT

What types of energy does the greenhouse use? Which type of energy is best for our environment?

PURPOSE:

- Identify the sun as a source of heat and light.
- Describe, using their observations, changes in heat and light from the sun over a period of time.
- Describe ways in which humans modify their behaviour to adapt to changes in temperature and sunlight during the day.
- Record relevant observations, findings, and measurements.
- Communicate the procedures and results of investigations.
- Plan investigations to answer questions posed.

MATERIALS:

- LM 3 for each child
- outdoor thermometer

TIME:

3 20–minute periods over the course of one day; repeated on other days

SKILL FOCUS:

observing, measuring, communicating

PLAY IT SAFE

For safety reasons, ensure the thermometer is not mercury-based. Caution children not to look directly at the sun.

" Weather changes during the day. "

GET STARTED

Pass a thermometer around for children to observe and describe. Encourage them to explain why we use thermometers. Demonstrate how to read the thermometer. Read and record the temperature in the classroom to model the numbers and degrees symbol.

Engage children in a discussion about weather changes by asking:

- Did anyone hear the weather forecast for today? What is it like outside? How might the weather change? Do you think the temperature stays the same all day? How could we find out?

WORK ON IT

USING PAGES 10 AND 11

After reading the text together have children examine the pictures. Begin by asking them to look carefully at the picture on page 10. Ask:

- What are the children doing? What do you see in the picture that helps you know what time of day it is? What type of weather is there? How does this picture compare to what it is like outdoors today?

Focus children's attention on the pictures on page 11, asking about each one:

- How can you tell that the children are in the same place? How can you tell that it is a different time of day? What do you suppose the children have found out? Do you think we will find out similar things when we go outdoors to see how weather changes?

BEYOND THE PAGE

Give each child a copy of LM 3. Take the children outside to make and record observations. After children have completed the three observations have them share their results. Ask:

- When was it the hottest? The coldest? What did you notice about the shadows? How would you describe how the sun appears to move?

COMMUNICATE

Have children take their sheets home to share, and ask them to record evening observations. The next day in class, children can describe the observations they recorded.

Repeat this activity for several days or once a week for several months. Children will begin to develop an appreciation for the changes that occur in a day.

Engage children in making predictions about the weather and thinking of ways to check them. Help them to prepare a plan for investigating their questions about weather observations.

ASSESSMENT OPPORTUNITY

Observe how children record and communicate the data they collect. Are they able to record information clearly? Can they refer to their recording to find information? Do they follow up at home as asked? Record your **observations** on AM 1, AM 2, or AM 3.

" Shadows change during the day. "

PURPOSE:

- Identify the sun as a source of heat and light.

- Describe, using their observations, changes in heat and light from the sun over a period of time.

- Ask questions about and identify needs or problems arising from observable events in the environment, and explore possible answers and solutions.

- Plan investigations to answer questions posed.

- Use appropriate vocabulary in describing investigations.

- Record relevant observations, findings, and measurements, by writing, drawing, making models or charts.

MATERIALS:

- chalk in different colours

TIME:

3 20–minute periods over the course of a day

SKILL FOCUS:

observing, comparing, inferring, measuring, communicating

PLAY IT SAFE

Caution children not to look directly at the sun.

GET STARTED

To begin, discuss shadows. Ask:

- What do you know about shadows? When do you see them outside? Are they always there? When have you seen your own shadow? What can you tell us about it?

Through discussion establish that we see shadows when an object blocks the path of light. When light comes from a light source, such as the sun, and a person stands in front of the path of that light, a shadow forms.

WORK ON IT

USING PAGES 12 AND 13

On a sunny day, find a safe place outdoors where children can trace their shadows onto asphalt. It is best to do this activity at least three times at two- or three-hour intervals during the day.

Before going outdoors have the children look at and discuss the pages. Make sure children are clear about standing in the same spot each time they trace their shadows. Pair children and give each pair a piece of chalk. Engage them in making some predictions before going outdoors. Ask:

- What do you think your shadow will look like? Do you think it is always the same size? The same shape?

BEYOND THE PAGE

Have pairs of children trace their shadows. Make sure they mark the spot with their names so that it is easy to identify on the next visit. Before going indoors ask children to find the sun in the sky, but not by looking at it directly. Arrive at an agreement as to how to describe where the sun is in the sky and record this for children on a class recording sheet. Add to this recording each time you go outdoors to trace shadows. Give children different colours of chalk for each tracing.

COMMUNICATE

When the three tracings are complete, encourage the children to talk about what they observed. Ask:

- What did you find out about how your shadow changes? When was it the shortest? What was the position of the sun in the sky? The longest? What was the position of the sun in the sky?

Repeat this activity over several days to allow children to observe that they see the sun in predictable positions in the sky over the period of a day and that those positions influence the length and shape of their shadows.

Explain that your shadow changes because the position of the sun changes in the sky. The higher the sun is, the shorter your shadow is.

Record other questions that children have about shadows and how they move. Help children plan investigations to gather information and answer their questions.

ASSESSMENT OPPORTUNITY

As children work or before they go outdoors **ask them to predict** how their shadows will have changed. Encourage them to tell why they are making that prediction. Once outdoors encourage them to describe how the light is different from earlier in the day. Ask them where the heat and light outdoors comes from. Record your **observations**.

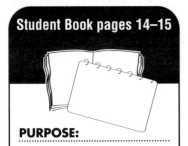

PURPOSE:

– Compare the characteristics of the seasons.

– Use units of time related to Earth's cycles.

– Identify outdoor human activities based on the seasons.

– Identify characteristics of clothing for different seasons and make appropriate decisions about clothing for different environmental conditions.

– Communicate with home.

MATERIALS:

• Family Letter B (optional)

TIME:

1 class period

SKILL FOCUS:

observing, comparing, inferring

At Home

GET STARTED

As a group, either look out the window or go outside. Invite children to describe any signs of the current season. Ask:

- How can you tell that right now it is (fall)? What do you suppose would be different if it were winter right now? Spring? Summer?

Next, focus children's attention on the time of day. Ask:

- How can you tell that it is now (morning)? What do you think would be different if it were night? Late afternoon?

WORK ON IT

USING PAGES 14 AND 15

As a class, choose one of the pictures on the page. Invite the children to give as much information about the season and the time of day as they can, and to explain their choices.

Send home the Student Book or Family Letter B and have children and their families complete the activity together. Alternatively, complete the activity in the classroom.

COMMUNICATE

Encourage children to bring to class family photos that were taken outdoors. Have children pass their photos around for others to see. You might add to the collection by including seasonal photographs cut from magazines or old calendars.

Once children have had a chance to explore, invite them to explain when they think the different photos were taken and to explain their reasons for choosing the season and time of day they do. You might direct children's attention to such aspects of the photos as the clothing people are wearing, how trees and flowers look, what activities people are doing, and what covers the ground.

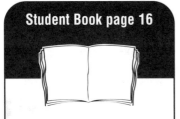

PURPOSE:

– Identify outdoor human activities that are based on the seasons.

– Identify characteristics of clothing worn in different seasons.

– Describe changes in the characteristics, behaviour, and location of living things that occur in seasonal cycles.

SKILL FOCUS:

observing

Look Back

WORK ON IT

USING PAGE 16

Together, read page 16 in the Student Book and ensure that everyone understands the task. Have children complete the activity on the page. Looking back through the book will help remind children about appropriate dress and activities for specific weather conditions.

ANSWERS

There are eight situations inappropriate for the weather. They are:
- person watering flowers
- skater in a bathing suit
- man barbequeing in short sleeves
- man in bathing suit and boots, hat, scarf, and mittens
- kid wearing snorkel gear
- girl in taxi wearing a bathing suit
- person in wheelchair wearing shorts
- woman entering building wearing sandals

COMMUNICATE

Invite children to share what they found, and to talk about what they learned about daily and seasonal cycles.

ASSESSMENT OPPORTUNITY

Provide children with a copy of AM 5 for self-assessment. Discuss children's answers with them individually, and store completed Assessment Masters in children's portfolios.

Demonstrate What You Know

PURPOSE:

– Assess children's learning.

MATERIALS:

- cards labelled with names of seasons
- large sheets of paper
- glue
- scissors
- LM 4 for each child

SKILL FOCUS:

observing, seriating, inferring

GET STARTED

Place cards with the names of the seasons on the chalkboard ledge in random order. Ask a volunteer to select one of the cards and post it on the chalkboard. Read it aloud together and then have volunteers select and post the appropriate cards in response to your directions to find what seasons come before and after. Discuss where to place the final card (at either end of the cycle) and why either choice is fine.

Read the cards in order several times. Have children close their eyes as you remove one card. Invite them to open their eyes and identify which season is missing and tell how they know.

ASSIGN THE TASK

Distribute LM 4. Ask children to describe what is happening in each picture. Explain they are to cut out the pictures and glue them in an order that makes sense. Provide large sheets of paper, glue, and scissors. When children have completed the gluing they should label each picture with a seasonal word. They can refer to the cards posted earlier.

Have children show and explain their ordering. Ask:

- How did you know that the picture showed fall? Summer and not spring?

Next, challenge children to draw people for each picture, either under the picture itself or on a separate sheet to be cut out and glued in place. Explain that the people must be dressed for the season and doing an activity that is appropriate for that time of year. Meet again for children to share their work when it is complete.

ASSESS THE TASK

The following will help you assess each child's learning about daily and seasonal cycles of change.

Performance Task Rubric	
Rubric	**Criteria**
Level 4	• child creates a sensible order for the pictures and labels each picture with the name of the correct season • child communicates, through words and pictures, an activity and clothing appropriate for each season
Level 3	• child creates a sensible order for the pictures but needs assistance to label each picture with the name of the correct season • child communicates, through words and pictures, an activity and clothing appropriate for 3 seasons
Level 2	• child needs assistance to put the pictures in order and to label each picture with the name of the correct season • child needs assistance to communicate, through words and pictures, an activity and clothing appropriate for some of the seasons
Level 1	• child has difficulty ordering the pictures and labelling the seasons • child cannot communicate an understanding of appropriate activities and clothing for the seasons

CHANGES ALL AROUND ME

Family Letter A

Dear Family,

We will be learning about the changes that occur during the day and during the seasons. We will look at how plants, animals, and humans adapt to and prepare for the changes that take place in different types of weather and during the four seasons.

Here are some activities that you can do at home to extend and reinforce our science curriculum. I hope that you enjoy them!

▶ Listen to the weather forecast in the morning together. Will it be warmer or cooler than yesterday? Discuss what your child should wear outdoors.

▶ Show your child the weather report and forecast in the newspaper. Together, read the times of sunrise and sunset. Do this daily for awhile. What do you notice? Is sunrise getting earlier or later? How is the time of sunset changing?

▶ Adopt a tree or plant near your home. Watch it regularly to see how it changes. Encourage your child to be a detective and to look for ways in which the tree has changed. How are the leaves the same? How are they changing?

▶ Discuss how you keep your home warm in the winter. Show your child the furnace and talk about how it heats your home. Point out vents, radiators, or baseboard heaters. Discuss the other ways that you try to keep your home warm. Talk about how you try to keep your home cool in the summer.

✂--

CHANGES ALL AROUND ME

Family Letter B

Dear Family,

We have begun discussing the following activity in the classroom, and hope you will enjoy completing the activity with your child.

Find photographs at home taken in different seasons and at different times of the day. Encourage your child to tell what season and time of day is shown in each photograph, and to explain how he or she knows.

Have your child bring one of the photographs to school to share with the class.

Copyright © 2000 Pearson Education Canada Inc.

Name: _____ Date: _____

Season: _____

My Seasons Journal

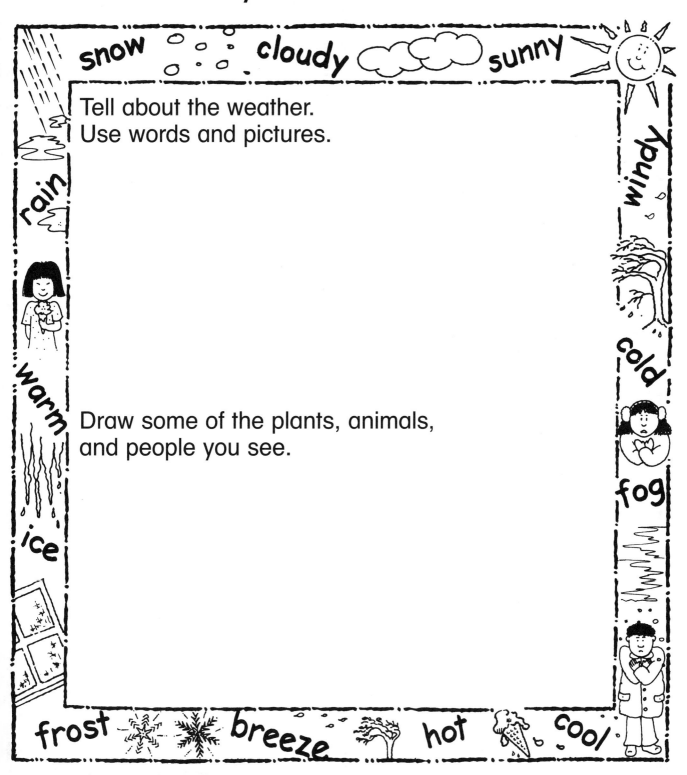

Tell about the weather.
Use words and pictures.

Draw some of the plants, animals,
and people you see.

Line Master 2

Filmstrip Template

——————— Changes All Around Me   Copyright © 2000 Pearson Education Canada Inc.

Name: _____   Date: _____

Season: _____

Today's Weather

Record the time of day and the temperature.

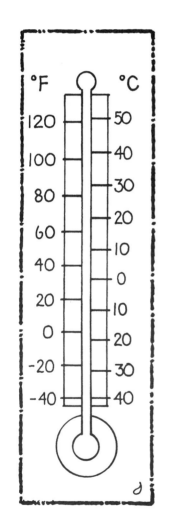

Time of Day
:
Temperature

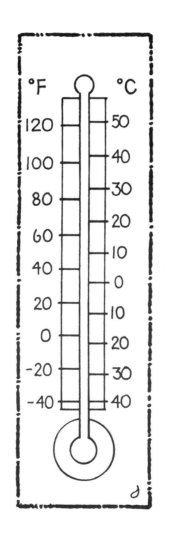

Time of Day
:
Temperature

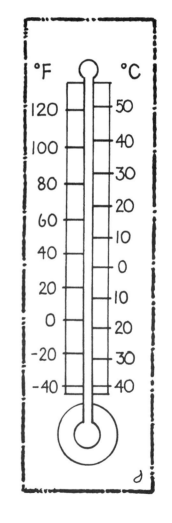

Time of Day
:
Temperature

Copyright © 2000 Pearson Education Canada Inc.

Copyright © 2000 Pearson Education Canada Inc.

It's Alive

UNIT OVERVIEW

In this unit children observe, compare, and define the basic needs and characteristics of living things.

- The unit begins with **children identifying** living and non-living things. They learn that all living things need food, water, and oxygen. Children then consider how living things grow and change.They compare their own growth to the growth of other living things and talk about the similarities and differences.

- **Children continue to explore** the needs and characteristics of living things as they observe and discuss pets. They investigate further by choosing an animal and researching what the animal needs to grow and develop.

- Finally **children investigate** the needs of seeds and plants. They examine a bean seed to learn how it develops into a plant, and they grow grass seed in different conditions. By changing the variables they observe first-hand what happens to plants when deprived of any of their basic needs — water, light, and air.

CONCEPT DEVELOPMENT AND OTHER ISSUES

If you have a classroom pet, this is an ideal time for the class to begin a research project to find out more about the characteristics and needs of the pet. You might collect relevant books, set up observation schedules, or make a visit to a veterinarian or pet store to gather information. If you do not have a pet, you might consider borrowing one from another classroom or having a child bring one (that resides in a terrarium or cage) from home for the children to care for in class for an extended period of time.

COLLECTING MATERIALS

Children will be looking carefully at bean seeds and will also be growing grass seed. You will need *bean seeds* and *grass seed* along with *potting soil, trays,* and *plastic cups for planting*. You may also wish to bring in some *plants for children to care for* and observe. The more experiences that children have caring for living things, the more they can appreciate the needs and characteristics of living things.

Unit Planner

ACTIVITY FOCUS ➜ CHILDREN:	TIME	MATERIALS
Ⓐ LAUNCH THE TOPIC ACTIVITY ▮▮		
state what they know about living things; create questions for inquiry and investigation	1 class period	paper, chart paper
Ⓑ ACTIVITY BANK ACTIVITIES ▮▮		
❶ **Pineapple Pieces** — identify the location and function of sense organs	⬆ **Take 5** ◖	pineapple or other fruit
❷ **Good Senses** — describe ways in which senses can protect and mislead		
❸ **Walk Like the Animals** — describe how animals move to meet their needs		pictures of animals moving
❹ **Animal Riddles** — describe how animals move to meet their needs	⬇	pictures of animals eating or acquiring food
❺ **The Caring Classroom** — describe how people adapt to loss or limitation of senses or abilities	⬆ **Take 30** ◑	
❻ **Eyes and Ears** — describe how people adapt to loss or limitation of senses or abilities; compare how humans and other animals use senses to meet needs	⬇	close-up pictures of animals, index cards, glue
❼ **Caring for Class Plants** — classify characteristics of plants using senses; identify needs of living things		various plants
❽ **Nature Table** — describe patterns observed in living things; identify a familiar plant or animal from a part of it	⬆ **Take Time** 🕐	magnifying lenses, microscope and slides, scales and rulers, writing and colouring materials, natural objects
❾ **Making a Living Thing Hotel** — identify needs of living things and explore ways of meeting those needs	⬇	animal or bug, jar with holes, food, water, journals, magnifying lenses, books
Ⓒ STUDENT BOOK/FLIP CHART BOOK ACTIVITIES ▮▮		
❶ **What living things can you find?** — *pages 2-3* compare basic needs of living things	1 to 2 class periods	chart paper, paper, writing and drawing materials
❷ **Animals are living things.** — *pages 4-5* identify body parts, sense organs, and ways that humans and animals move	2 to 3 class periods	animal pictures, glue, paper, drawing materials
❸ **Living things grow and change.** — *pages 6-7* describe and compare growth and change in humans and other living things.	1 class period	long strips of paper, scissors, glue, drawing materials
❹ **What do animals need to grow and stay healthy?** — *pages 8-9* identify needs of animals	2 class periods	paper, drawing materials, small pet with its home and food, magnifying lenses, recording tools, reference materials
❺ **Plants are living things.** — *pages 10-11* identify needs of plants	2 class periods	2 different plants, weeds or wildflowers for each group, chart paper, marker, magnifying lenses
❻ **What does a bean seed need to grow?** — *pages 12-13* identify needs of plants and effects of withholding needs	2 to 3 class periods	magnifying lenses, measuring tools, small planter, potting soil, spray bottle, water, bean seeds, spoons
❼ **At Home** — *pages 14-15* identify needs of plants	equivalent to 1 class period	
❽ **Look Back** — *page 16* reflect on and synthesize what they know	1 class period	
Ⓓ DEMONSTRATE WHAT YOU KNOW TASK ▮▮		
❶ draw a living thing and describe its needs and characteristics	1 class period	chart paper, drawing and writing materials

ACTIVITY DESCRIPTION ➤ CHILDREN:	LINE MASTERS	ASSESSMENT
- write/draw what they know about plants, animals, people; create a 'Know/Wonder/Learned' chart	Family Letter Master A	
- use senses to describe a fruit		
- answer questions about how senses help us		
- move like an animal		
- guess animals from riddles about their characteristics		
- identify ways to support people with limited use of senses		
- describe sensory organs and demonstrate how they can help		
- care for a plant in class		
- observe and classify living and non-living things		portfolio
- create a habitat and care for a small creature		observation, interview
- create a bulletin board display of living and non-living things		observation
- sort pictures of animals by a variety of characteristics	LM 1	portfolio
- sort pictures to show the growth sequence of living things	LM 2	observation
- care for a pet in the classroom		observation, interview
- examine plants and record observations	LM 3	observation, portfolio
- grow a plant from seeds and record observations		observation, interview
-with their families, grow a plant from a potato	Family Letter Master B	
- identify plants and animals from close-up pictures of their parts		
- draw a living thing and describe its needs and characteristics	LM 4	rubric

PLANNING AHEAD

TEACHER RESOURCES

Hickman, Pamela. Bugwise. Toronto: Kids Can Press, 1990.

Nickelsburg, Janet. Nature Activities for Early Childhood. Menlo Park: Addison Wesley Publishers Ltd., 1976.

Suzuki, David and Hehner, Barbara. Looking at Plants. Toronto: Stoddart Publishing Co. 1985.

BOOKS FOR CHILDREN

Burton, Marilee Robin. Tail Toes Eyes Ears Nose. New York: Harper, 1998.

Ehlert, Lois. Growing Vegetable Soup. New York: Harcourt Brace Jovanovich, 1987.

Lotteridge, Celia B. One Watermelon Seed. Toronto: Oxford University Press, 1987.

Mason, Adrienne. Living Things. Toronto: Kids Can Press, 1997.

Morton, Alexandra. Siwiti: A Whale's Story. Victoria, B.C.: Orca Book Publishers, 1992.

WEB SITES

Animal Planet: http://animal.discovery.com

The Food Guide: www.hc-sc.gc.ca/ hppb/nutrition/pube/foodguid/ foodguide.html

CD-ROMS

Exploring Science: Seeds from Seedlings by Queue. Win/Mac

My Amazing Human Body Ages 6-10 by DK Multimedia. Win/Mac

Zookeeper by Davidson. Win/Mac

VIDEOS

Animal Café, B.C. Learning Connection Inc.

Minnie's Science Field Trips: The San Diego Zoo, Magic Lantern Communications Ltd.

Looking at Birds, B.C. Learning Connection Inc.

Cross-Curricular Overview

LINK TO...
SOCIAL STUDIES UNIT

MY FAMILY AND FRIENDS

Any time after Activity 3, consider teaching Activity 6 from **My Family and Friends** in Ginn Social Studies. In this activity, children discuss how the rules for and responsibilities of family members change over time. Discuss life cycles with children, explaining that, for living things, our bodies aren't the only things that change over time. Our abilities and interests change as well.

I'LL BE THE SOUND, YOU BE THE MOVEMENT

Curriculum Link: *Drama and Dance*
Use any time after: Activity 2

Purpose
- Describe some basic ways in which the body can be used in space and time.
- Demonstrate control of their bodies when moving like different objects and animals.

Get Started
Invite the children to brainstorm as many animals as they can. Record their responses, then have one volunteer at a time demonstrate the sound of any animal of his or her choice. Ask:

- How would you move to show that animal?

Ask the children to choose one animal to begin the activity.

Work On It
Divide the class in half. Designate one group to be the animal's movement and the other group to be the animal's sound. On a signal from you, have the movement group move like that animal. On the next signal, have them freeze. On another signal from you, the sound group can make the sound. On the next signal, they stop. At the next set of signals, both groups can start and stop together. Have the groups change roles and repeat the activity.

Communicate
Designate roles to the children again, then have them choose another animal. On your signal, have the groups move and do the sound at the same time, again stopping on your signal.

Begin a series of animal movements and sounds, by continuing to add an animal and having the children repeat the activity for each animal in an "add-on" fashion. Children may enjoy singing "Old MacDonald Had a Farm," then performing the movements and noises of the chosen animals.

WHO'S THAT BABY

Curriculum Link: *Health and Physical Education*
Use any time after: Activity 3

Purpose
- Describe simple life cycles of humans.

Materials
- baby picture of yourself
- baby picture of each child
- Bristol board
- paper and drawing materials

Get Started

Ask families for a baby picture of each child, labelled on the back. Show the children a baby picture of yourself, but don't identify it. Ask:
- Who do you think this is? How do you know?

When the group guesses correctly, explain that humans can change a lot over time. Human bodies grow bigger, their skin and hair changes, and they learn to do different things.

Work On It

Post children's baby pictures on a large piece of Bristol board. Keep a record for yourself of who is in each picture. Point to each picture and ask:
- Who do you think this is? How do you know?

When the group guesses correctly, write the child's name below the picture.

Communicate

Challenge children to draw a self portrait. Invite children to share their work with the class and to describe at least one difference between the way they looked as a baby and the way they look now. You may want to post children's self-portraits and baby pictures together.

LIVING THINGS ART GALLERY

Curriculum Link: *Visual Arts*
Use any time after: Activity 5

Purpose
- Make artistic choices in their work, using at least one of the elements of design specified for this grade.
- Produce two- and three-dimensional works of art that communicate thoughts and feelings.

Materials
- art materials for painting, sculpting, collage, and so on

Get Started

Review with children the various charts and displays of living things they have helped created throughout the unit. Ask:
- What living things do we know? How do we know they are alive?

Work On It

Provide children with a variety of art materials. Challenge them to choose a living thing and create an art work that depicts it. Encourage children to think of the medium that would best suit what they want to show — they may wish to paint or draw, make a sculpture from modelling clay, make a torn-paper collage, collect rubbings and put them together to create their art work, and so on.

Communicate

Invite children to share their completed works with the class. Encourage them to describe the living thing they chose, what medium they chose to create their art work, and why they think that medium was the best way for them to share what they wanted to share. Set up a classroom art gallery to display the children's art works.

A LAUNCH THE TOPIC

Create a three-column chart. Label the columns People, Animals, Plants. Read the headings aloud. Then ask the children to tell things that they know for sure about people, animals, and plants. Record children's statements. Provide children with paper and ask them to illustrate one of these statements or any other that they think of. Post the illustrations around the chart.

People	Animals	Plants
they eat food	there are lots of kinds	they need water
boys and girls	some can fly	flowers are pretty
different colours of eyes	some have fur	trees give shade

KEEP IT GOING

Invite the children to look at the chart. Ask:

- Did we say any of the same things for people, animals, and plants?

Underline the comments that appear in more than one column. Keep this chart posted and encourage children to add to it as you work through the activities in this unit.

As you begin this unit, send home Family Letter A. Encourage families to do some of the activities suggested to enhance children's learning about living things.

B ACTIVITY BANK

1 PINEAPPLE PIECES

PURPOSE: –Identify the location and function of each sense organ.

MATERIALS: pineapple or another fruit

Engage children in a discussion about their senses. Ask:

- What part of our body helps us see? Hear? Smell? Touch? Taste? How do our senses help us?

To illustrate that our senses help us acquire information, pass around the pineapple and ask:

- What information do you know about this by looking at it? Smelling it? Touching it?

Prompt further observations by cutting open the pineapple. Consider giving children a small piece of the fruit to taste and describe. Be aware of food allergies. Even smelling a food may trigger an allergic reaction.

2 GOOD SENSES

PURPOSE: –Describe ways in which the senses can both protect and mislead.

Ask the children a variety of questions that focus on the senses. For example:

- How do you know when a pot on the stove is hot? Do you actually have to touch it to find out?

- What lets you know there is a fire burning?

- How do you know when an emergency vehicle is approaching?

- What senses can you use when it is dark?

- When you have a cold, is it easier or harder to smell things?

- What do you do to make sure you don't get hurt crossing the street?

- How can you tell when milk has gone sour? Should you taste it or smell it first?

Invite the children to come up with other ways our senses protect us.

3 WALK LIKE THE ANIMALS

PURPOSE: –Describe the different ways in which animals move to meet their needs.

MATERIALS: pictures of animals moving

Explain to the children that animals move in different ways. Display pictures of animals moving and invite the children to identify the animal by the way it moves (crawl, swim, run, fly, jump, walk, climb). Then ask:

- Do any of these animals move in more than one way? (birds, monkeys, bears) What different things are they doing when they move that way? (a hawk flies to escape danger, find food; a robin walks to find food, to look for material to build a nest).

Select one animal at a time and ask volunteers to move like that animal.

4 ANIMAL RIDDLES

PURPOSE: –Describe the different ways in which animals move to meet their needs.

MATERIALS: pictures of animals eating or acquiring food

Explain to the children that animals need food, just like they do, to stay alive. Different animals get food in different ways. For example, a cow grazes on grass, a squirrel holds its food in its two front paws, and a lion runs quickly and attacks its prey with its sharp claws and teeth.

Post three or four pictures at a time and present a riddle that includes the ways one of the animals moves to get or eat its food. For example: I am green and catch insects with my long tongue. Who am I? I have a shell and hide in it when I am scared. Who am I?

Encourage the children to offer riddles for others to guess. The next time you play, you might focus on how young animals get their food. For example, newborn alligators, frogs, and many fish get their own food, while most newborn birds eat food brought by their parents. Mammals drink milk from their mother.

5 THE CARING CLASSROOM

PURPOSE: –Describe ways in which people adapt to the loss or limitation of sensory or physical activity.

Challenge the children to imagine what it would be like to be unable to see or hear. On the board, list the difficulties children suggest and discuss ways they think they could overcome these difficulties. Ask:

- How do dog guides help blind people? Does anyone know of other things that help blind people in our seeing world?

Children may also know of things that support hearing impaired people, such as closed captioning on televisions. Ask:

- How would you change the shelves (hooks, desks, books) in our classroom so that a visually impaired child could still find things? How could we help a hearing impaired child know what we were learning about and when it was time for recess?

Point out that people must rely on their other senses when one sense is impaired. Ask:

- How do dog guides help blind people? Does anyone know of other things that help blind people in our seeing world?

Children may also know of things that support hearing impaired people, such as closed captioning on televisions.

⑥ EYES AND EARS

PURPOSE: – Describe ways in which people adapt to the loss or limitations of sensory or physical ability.

– Compare ways in which humans and other animals use their senses to meet their needs.

MATERIALS: close-up pictures of animals
index cards
glue

Explain to the children that animals, including us, use their senses to gather information. Animals use their senses to find food, find or create shelter, and protect themselves. Show close-up pictures of different animals. Focus on one sense organ at a time. For example, ask:

- What do you know about your eyes? When is it easiest to see? Hardest? What do people do if they have a poor sense of sight?

Show close-up pictures of different animal eyes. Encourage the children to describe the different types of eyes. Discuss where they are positioned on the animal's head and why. (Animals with eyes in the front tend to be hunters. Large eyes usually indicate a nocturnal animal. Animals with eyes on the side of their heads tend to be hunted and need to see on both sides to spot danger.)

On another occasion focus on ears. Have children cover their ears with their hands as you say something quietly, then loudly. Have them compare what they heard. Ask:

- What do people do when they have a poor sense of hearing?

Repeat, this time having children cup their hand around their ear. Explain that the outside of the ear catches sounds. When children make this part bigger with their hand they may hear better. Use the pictures to show close-ups of different animal ears. Discuss why big ears are helpful to animals and why some animals have no ears at all.

⑦ CARING FOR CLASS PLANTS

PURPOSE: – Classify characteristics of plants by using their senses.

– Select and use appropriate tools to increase their capacity to observe.

– Ask questions about and identify some needs of living things.

MATERIALS: various plants (including fast-growing plants such as seeds and slow-growing plants such as cacti)

Bring in several different kinds of plants for the children to observe and care for. Ask:

- How are the plants the same? Different?

Emphasize characteristics such as size, shape, texture of the leaves, and the height of the plant. Ask:

■ What do the plants need to stay alive?

Encourage the children to help you find a good place for the plants in the classroom. Engage them in setting up a routine in which they assume responsibility for the care of the plants.

8 NATURE TABLE

PURPOSE:
– Describe patterns that they have observed in living things.

– Select and use appropriate tools to increase their capacity to observe.

– Identify a familiar animal or plant from seeing only a part of it.

MATERIALS:
magnifying lenses
microscope and slides
scales and rulers
writing and colouring materials
natural objects (flowers, leaves, rocks, pine cones, turtle shell)

Place a variety of natural objects at a centre along with observation tools, after demonstrating their use. Encourage the children to observe the items and record their observations. Challenge them to look for and describe patterns they observe, and identify the items that are living, non-living, or once living. For those items that are a part of a larger object (for example, a petal or a leaf), invite the children to identify the whole from observing the part and to draw a diagram that shows the whole item, including the part they observed.

9 MAKING A LIVING THING HOTEL

PURPOSE:
Select and use appropriate tools to increase their capacity to observe; ask questions about and identify some needs of living things, and explore possible answers to these questions and ways of meeting these needs; plan an investigation to answer some of these questions or find ways of meeting these needs; use appropriate vocabulary in describing their investigations, explorations, and observations; identify ways in which individuals can maintain a healthy environment for themselves and for other living things.

MATERIALS:
an animal or bug (a caterpillar is ideal)
jar with holes
food and water
journals
magnifying lenses
books

In warm weather, take the children outside and ask:

■ What do the things living outside need to stay healthy? If we bring a living thing inside, what will we need?

Based on their answers, encourage the children to think about a "hotel" for a small living creature. While still outside, ask:

■ What do you think the (spider) needs to live? What do you see that might be food for it? What kind of place does it need to live?

Encourage the children to gather materials from the area where the creature is found and build the hotel. Place the small creature in the container, securing a mesh covering over the top. Ask:

■ Does the creature have everything it needs to live? How will we make sure the hotel remains a safe and healthy home?

Provide magnifying lenses, recording tools, and reference materials to prompt children to observe their visitor, ask questions, and gather information. Provide time for children to share their observations, discoveries, and recordings with one another. After a day or two, return the visitor to its natural environment.

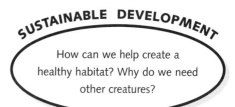

SUSTAINABLE DEVELOPMENT

How can we help create a healthy habitat? Why do we need other creatures?

Student Book pages 2–3

PURPOSE:

– Compare the basic needs of humans with the needs of other living things.

MATERIALS:

- chart paper
- paper
- writing and drawing materials

TIME:

1 to 2 class periods

SKILL FOCUS:

classifying, observing

" What living things can you find? "

GET STARTED

Engage children in a discussion about living things by focusing on children themselves. Ask:

- I know that you are all alive, but how do we know? What do you think all living things need?

Through this discussion establish that living things grow, move, breathe, eat, and drink. Ask children to think about non-living things. Give an example, such as a balloon, and ask why it isn't a living thing. Challenge children to look around the classroom and ask:

- What other living things are in our room? Non-living things?

List the objects on a chart labeled: Living and Non-Living.

Provide children with a sheet of paper. Have them fold it in half, then draw a living thing on one half and a non-living thing on the other half. Post the headings "Living Things" and "Non-Living Things" on a bulletin board. Have children cut their page in half and post their recordings under the corresponding head.

Point out that there are pictures of both animals and plants in the "Living Things" section of the bulletin board. Ask interested children to help rearrange the pictures to create a group of plants and a group of animals. As you discuss each group, ask:

- How are you the same as these animals? These plants? What things do you all need to stay alive?

WORK ON IT

USING PAGES 2 AND 3

Encourage children to describe the scene in the book. Say, "We have identified lots of living things on our chart. What other ones can you find on these pages?" List their responses under Living Things. Ask:

- How do you know it is alive? Which of the living things are animals? Plants? What do all living things need?

Have children find something in the picture that is not alive. List their responses under Non-Living. Ask:

- How do you know it isn't alive?

Interested children can draw pictures of living and non-living things that they see in this scene to add to the bulletin board.

BEYOND THE PAGE

Take children on a hunt through the classroom, school, and playground to find other living and non-living things to add to the class bulletin board.

COMMUNICATE

Once back in class have children draw pictures of their observations, and add these to the bulletin board display.
During these discussions, the placement of things that were once alive may come up. You can create a third category and call it "Once Alive." Point out that only living things can die.

EXTENSION

Encourage children to keep searching for living and non-living things — inside and outside their homes, at the park, or on a drive. Provide drawing materials and picture collections so children can add to the bulletin board.

ASSESSMENT OPPORTUNITY

Listen to the responses and ideas that children offer during discussion. Are they able to distinguish between living and non-living things? Can they describe the needs of living things? AM 1 can be used to note how children are able to identify the needs of living things.

PURPOSE:

- Identify major parts of the human body and describe their functions.

- Identify the location and function of each sense organ.

- Identify and describe common characteristics of humans and other animals that they have observed, and identify variations in these characteristics.

- Classify characteristics of animals and plants by using the senses.

MATERIALS:

- animal pictures
- copies of LM 1
- glue
- drawing materials
- paper

TIME:

2 to 3 class periods

SKILL FOCUS:

observing, classifying

" Animals are living things. "

GET STARTED

Get children thinking about the characteristics of their own bodies by playing Simon Says. Use instructions that help children identify body parts, sense organs, and ways of moving. For example: Simon says slither slowly on your stomach, Simon says point to the part of your body that you use for breathing, or Simon says cover the part of your body that you use to (see, hear, smell, touch).

Discuss the characteristics of the children's own bodies and how they help them meet their needs by asking:

- How do you get your food? What parts of your body help you eat? Breathe? What are some different ways you move? What parts of your body do you use to move?

WORK ON IT

USING PAGES 4 AND 5

Invite children to identify the animals on the page, then describe and compare them.

- How are these animals alike? Different?

Focus their attention on movement, appearance, and behaviour, using questions like these:

- How do these animals look the same? Different? How do these animals get their food? Which parts of their bodies help them? How do these animals move? Why do they move that way? How are you the same as these animals? Different?

BEYOND THE PAGE

Provide children with animal pictures cut from LM 1 and from other sources. Encourage them to create a set of pictures that are the same in at least one way. They can glue their set on paper and draw other animals that belong to the set. As children work, encourage them to describe how the animals in their set are the same and how they are different.

COMMUNICATE

Invite children to present their completed sets to the class and have others guess their sorting rule. As a class, consider some of the different ways in which the animals were sorted. Record the rules on a chart entitled We Sorted Animals By... . Invite interested children to create additional sets.

ASSESSMENT OPPORTUNITY

The recordings children make are good **portfolio** entries. They can give you insight into children's ability to identify and classify living things. Ask children to explain their decisions to you and note their thinking directly on their recordings. AM 4 is provided to help track portfolio entries.

PURPOSE:

– Describe some basic changes in humans as they grow, and compare changes in humans with changes in other living things.

MATERIALS:

- copies of LM 2
- long strips of paper
- scissors
- glue
- drawing materials

TIME:

1 class period

SKILL FOCUS

comparing, seriating

" Living things grow and change. "

GET STARTED

A couple of days before you begin this lesson, ask children to bring in baby photos and recent photos of themselves. Invite children to present their photos to the class. Ask them how they have grown and changed since they were a baby.

Ask what they like about being their current age and what they can do now that they couldn't do as a baby or toddler. Record their responses. Then focus their attention on the changes in humans over time by giving them the strip of people cut from LM 2. Ask children to cut out each picture and to order the pictures on a long strip of paper to show the growth sequence. Before children glue the pictures ask them to draw themselves in the sequence at their current age and, if they wish, as what they think they will look like as an adult. Some children might like to label each stage.

Use the sequenced pictures to prompt observation and discussion. To focus on specific characteristics of each stage, ask:

- When you were a (baby), how did you move? What did you eat? How did you get the food you needed? What sounds did you make? What did you look like?

To compare different stages, ask:

- How does the toddler move? How has that changed from when she was a baby? Why? What foods can she eat? How has the way the toddler eats changed? Why? How have the sounds she makes changed? How can these new sounds help her?

WORK ON IT

USING PAGES 6 AND 7

Encourage children to describe the changes in the way the puppy grows. Have them focus on such changes as movement, sound, and eating and drinking habits.

Ask children to place their ordered pictures of the human's growth beside the page. Ask:

- How is the (newborn baby) the same as the (newborn puppy)? How is it different?

BEYOND THE PAGE

Provide children with the rest of the strips cut from LM 2. Invite them to cut the strips apart and to put them in order to show the growth sequence for each animal.

COMMUNICATE

Meet as a large group and have children describe the sequence they have created. Engage them in thinking of words to describe the changes they see in the pictures. Ask:

- What do you think would be a good caption for each frame?

Through discussion establish complete descriptions. Capture the discussion by recording the group's decisions on chart paper. End by reading the recording aloud.

ASSESSMENT OPPORTUNITY

Listen to the descriptions children give and **watch** to see how they order the pictures they are given. Can they describe and compare the changes in living things as they grow? Note your observations on AM 1, AM 2, or AM 3.

PURPOSE:

– Identify ways in which individuals can maintain a healthy environment for themselves and for other living things.

– Ask questions about and identify some needs of living things, and explore possible answers to these questions and ways of meeting these needs.

– Use appropriate vocabulary in describing their observations.

– Plan investigations to answer some of these questions or find ways of meeting these needs.

MATERIALS:

• paper
• drawing materials
• small pet with its home and food
• magnifying lenses
• recording tools
• reference materials

TIME:

2 class periods

SKILL FOCUS:

observing, communicating

"" # What do animals need to grow and stay healthy? ""

GET STARTED

Engage children in a discussion of what they need to grow and stay healthy. Establish the need for nutritious foods, plenty of liquids, exercise, fresh air, cleanliness, safe behaviour, and a protective home.

Then provide children with paper and drawing materials. Invite them to draw themselves in a situation where they are helping themselves to stay healthy. Have related books, including Canada's Food Guide to Healthy Eating, on display. Encourage children to share their recordings.

Post the heading, How We Keep Healthy, and display their work.

WORK ON IT

USING PAGES 8 AND 9

Before opening the book, ask:

■ What do you think all living things need to stay healthy and alive?

Record the children's responses. Have them look at the pages. Ask:

■ What do these pets need to stay healthy? What else might they need?

Establish through discussion that animals need food, water, exercise, air to breathe, and a clean and protective home. Children who have a pet can describe how they care for it.

BEYOND THE PAGE

Arrange to have a small pet (fish, mouse, rabbit, caterpillar, frog, hamster) from another classroom or from a child's home visit the classroom, for several weeks if possible. Explain that the pet is a living thing and it must be cared for so it stays healthy and safe. Discuss how they will do this. Focus their attention on the routines needed to care for the pet by asking such questions as:

■ Who will feed the pet? How can we make sure that it gets the right amount of food? Water? Exercise? What will we do with the pet on the weekends?

When the animal is comfortable with its new surroundings, encourage the children to observe its characteristics, movements, and behaviours. Provide magnifying lenses, recording tools, and reference materials, and prompt children to observe, ask questions, and gather information about their visitor.

COMMUNICATE

Children may have questions about the needs of other animals. Invite them to pose questions and decide how to investigate those questions. Help them, if necessary, to gather reference materials, prepare an interview, or bring another pet to class. Children may wish to share their information through a poster, a booklet, a model, or an oral presentation.

EXTENSION

Arrange a field trip to a farm or a zoo so children can learn about the needs and characteristics of different kinds of animals.

ASSESSMENT OPPORTUNITY

Listen to children's comments and **ask** them **questions** to determine whether they have an understanding of basic needs of living things. Can the child ask a clear question? Can the child follow through and get information? How does the child tell others what he or she found out? You can note children's research skills on AM 1, AM 2, or AM 3.

SUSTAINABLE DEVELOPMENT

What do animals need to live and stay healthy? How can we help?

PURPOSE:

– Describe patterns that they have observed in living things.

– Select and use appropriate tools to increase their capacity to observe.

– Identify some needs of living things, and explore ways of meeting these needs.

– Record relevant observations.

– Communicate the procedures and results of investigations.

MATERIALS:

• 2 different types of plants (for example, an herb and a cactus)
• plants of some kind for each group
• chart paper
• marker
• magnifying lenses
• LM 3

TIME:

2 class periods

SKILL FOCUS:

observing, communicating

PLAY IT SAFE

Caution children not to eat or harm any plants.

" Plants are living things. "

GET STARTED

Provide children with a magnifying lens and recording materials. Take them outdoors to observe plants, and to record by drawing, writing, measuring, and making rubbings.

Children might break open seed pods or shells or smell flowers and carefully feel the different parts of living plants. Encourage them to collect parts of plant (seeds, cones, leaves, branches) from the ground. Use them for further discussion and observation.

Back in the classroom, ask:
• Where did we see plants growing? (sidewalk cracks, up walls, gardens) How do they get water?

Have children share their observations and recordings.

WORK ON IT

USING PAGES 10 AND 11

Encourage children to name and describe each plant on the page. Ask:
• How are these plants alike? Different? How are the (stems) alike? Different? What other plant parts do you see?

BEYOND THE PAGE

Remind the children that they have learned that animals need food, water, air, and a healthy, safe place to live. Plants also need certain things to grow and stay alive. Present at least two different types of plants and ask:
• What do these plants need to stay healthy and alive? (soil, water, and sunlight) How do people take care of plants on a farm? In a garden? How do wild plants stay healthy and alive?

Have children look carefully at the plants and describe their similarities and differences. Through the discussion emphasize characteristics such as plant parts (stem, root, leaves, flower, fruit, seed), size, shape, and colour.

COMMUNICATE

Place plants and magnifying lenses at several work areas. Give individuals paper and drawing materials. Encourage them to draw the plant including as many of the observable features as possible. When children's drawings are complete meet as a group so children can display and describe their observations. Ask:
• What words would you like to use to label your drawings?

List suggested words and encourage children to add labels to their recordings. Interested children may want to observe another plant and record their observations.

EXTENSION

Provide children with pictures cut from LM 3 and invite them to create a set of pictures that is alike in at least one way. Challenge them to find other ways to sort the plant pictures.

ASSESSMENT OPPORTUNITY

Observe whether children are using the tools appropriately. Can they describe the changes as the plants grow? The children's observation booklets are excellent **portfolio** entries as they indicate how a child communicates observations and measures over time.

"What does a bean seed need to grow?"

PURPOSE:

- Select and use appropriate tools to increase capacity to observe.

- Ask questions about and identify some needs of living things, explore answers and ways of meeting needs.

- Plan investigations to answer questions or find ways of meeting needs.

- Use appropriate vocabulary in describing their investigations, explorations, and observations.

- Record relevant observations.

- Communicate procedures and results of investigations.

MATERIALS:

- magnifying lenses
- measuring tools
- small planter
- potting soil
- spray bottle
- water
- bean seeds
- spoons

TIME:

2 to 3 class periods; daily observation over a few weeks

SKILL FOCUS:

observing, predicting, measuring, experimenting, communicating, controlling variables

GET STARTED

Engage children in a discussion about their previous experiences with growing things. Then give the children two bean seeds and give them time to examine them with a magnifying lens. Discuss and compare the seeds. Then have the children predict what would happen if one seed was soaked in water.

After they share their predictions, have them place one seed in a shallow dish of water overnight. The next day, review their predictions before examining the wet seed with magnifying lenses and comparing it to the dry one (wet seed may be bigger, outer coat slippery and wrinkled, starting to sprout). Children might be able to look inside and see the baby leaf and root beginning to grow. Ask them to make a recording of the dry seed and the wet seed by drawing or writing.

WORK ON IT

USING PAGES 12 AND 13

Remind children that they have discussed how people and animals grow and change. Plants grow and change too. Look at the pages and ask:

- What materials do you need? What will you do first? Why will you place the seed by the window? Why do you need to give it water? What do you think would happen if the bean seed didn't have the things it needed to grow?

Record these predictions. Then place all of the materials in a central location. Have each group plant three containers of bean seeds: one in a sunny location, watering it lightly each day; one in a dark place with water and air; and one in a sunny location with no water.

BEYOND THE PAGE

Over the next two weeks have children observe their bean seeds every few days. Provide magnifying lenses and measuring tools to enhance their observations. Make sure that children record and date their observations (a date stamp is helpful). Each entry can describe the growth of beans in each of the three situations.

Encourage children to tell about these observations. Hearing about one another's work will expose children to new possibilities for observation, such as the colour of the sprouts, the number of sprouts, or the length of the sprout.

COMMUNICATE

Children can share their work once they have made several observations. Questions like these will promote discussion:

- Which plants seem to be the healthiest? Do you think we have seen that plants need water and light to grow well?

Encourage children to continue to pose questions related to growing plants. Ask:

- What else would you like to grow? What do you think you will need?

Record children's interests and questions. They might want to grow other seeds, try different watering schedules, grow plants under grow lights, or use plant food. Help children make a plan and collect the needed materials.

ASSESSMENT OPPORTUNITY

Listen to the questions that children pose. Encourage them to suggest ways to answer their questions and watch to see how they follow through with the plan. Do children show an understanding of what seeds need to grow? Are they able to communicate their findings clearly? Record your **observations** on AM 1 and AM 3.

SUSTAINABLE DEVELOPMENT

Why is it good to have plants around us? How do they help the environment?

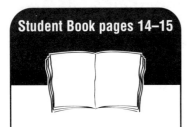

PURPOSE:

– Ask questions and identify some needs of living things, and explore possible answers to these questions and ways of meeting these needs.

– Record relevant observations.

– Communicate the procedures and results of investigations for specific purposes

– Communicate with home.

MATERIALS:

• Family Letter B

SKILL FOCUS:

observing, communicating

At Home

GET STARTED

Play a game of 20 Questions with the children, where the item you are thinking of is a potato. Say:

- I am thinking of a vegetable. You can only ask me questions that I can answer with yes or no. Can you guess what vegetable I am thinking of?

Give children hints only if they appear to get impatient with their progress.

WORK ON IT

USING PAGES 14 AND 15

Once children have guessed that you are thinking of a potato, explain that the potato is from a family of plants called tubers. A tuber is a root-like structure from which potatoes grow.

Ask children to examine pages 14 and 15. Together, review the outlined procedure for growing potatoes without seeds.

Send home the Student Book or Family Letter B so that children and their families can grow a potato at home. Alternatively, complete this activity in class. You might also consider bringing in crocus, tulip, or daffodil bulbs, inviting children to examine them, and then planting them.

COMMUNICATE

After children have had a chance to grow a plant from a potato without a seed, encourage them to tell about what they noticed. Sharing observations in class will maintain interest in the project and inspire others who have not tried it. You might ask questions such as these:

- What did you notice? What did you do to help your potato grow? How did your potato change as it started to grow? How did the potato grow a plant without a seed? Where did the plant grow from? How did the plant grow? What did it need to grow? Do you know of other plants that can be grown without seeds?

PURPOSE:

– Recognize physical characteristics of living things.

SKILL FOCUS:

observing

Look Back

WORK ON IT

USING PAGE 16

Together, read page 16 in the Student Book and ensure that everyone understands the task. Have children complete the activity on the page.

ANSWERS

The children will find:
- a daisy (page 2)
- the owl (page 5)
- the dog (page 6)
- a goldfish (page 8)
- a dandelion (page 11)

COMMUNICATE

Invite children to share what they found, and to talk about what they learned about living things.

ASSESSMENT OPPORTUNITY

Provide children with a copy of AM 5 for self-assessment. Discuss children's answers with them individually, and store completed Assessment Masters in children's portfolios.

Demonstrate What You Know

PURPOSE:

- Assess children's learning.

MATERIALS:

- chart paper
- LM 4
- drawing and writing materials

SKILL FOCUS:

communicating, interpreting

GET STARTED

Print the title Living Things on chart paper. Ask:

- What living things can you think of?

Print children's responses. Make sure there are at least ten entries. Play the game Twenty Questions. Ask a volunteer to choose one of the living things from the chart and whisper it to you, but not share it with the class. Invite the other children to ask questions that can be answered only with a yes or no. Their goal is to gain enough information to be able to tell which living thing was selected. You may need to model some questions to get children started (for example, Can your living thing move? Is your living thing a plant? Does your living thing fly?). Repeat so that many children have the opportunity to ask questions.

ASSIGN THE TASK

Distribute LM 4 and invite children to choose any living thing to draw. Make sure that children understand that they must begin by drawing their living things with as much detail as possible. When the drawing is complete, they can draw or write to describe it and tell what it needs to survive. Before they begin, you might want to brainstorm and record a list of words that children think they will need to complete the task.

Challenge children to use their recordings to play the game Twenty Questions as they did at the beginning of this activity.

ASSESS THE TASK

The following rubric will help you assess each child's learning about living things.

Performance Task Rubric	
Rubric	**Criteria**
Level 4	• child creates a detailed drawing of a living thing • child provides a detailed description of a living thing or asks questions that demonstrate an understanding of the basic needs and characteristics of living things
Level 3	• child creates a complete but not detailed drawing of a living thing • child provides some description of a living thing or asks at least two questions that demonstrate an understanding of the basic needs and characteristics of living things
Level 2	• child draws a living thing • child requires assistance to describe a living thing or asks one question that demonstrates an understanding of the basic needs and characteristics of living things
Level 1	• child does not complete a drawing of a living thing • child does not complete a description and is unable to ask questions or identify basic needs of living things

IT'S ALIVE

Family Letter Ⓐ

Dear Family,

We are learning about living things. We will be discussing what they need and how they grow and change, and finding a variety of living things in and around our school. We will also grow plants from seeds.

Visit the library and collect books and resources on animals and plants that interest your child. Encourage your child to ask questions, make observations, and talk about the information gathered.

Here are some other activities that you can do at home to extend and reinforce our science curriculum. I hope that you enjoy them!

▶ Ask your child to help plan a healthy meal for the family using the four basic food groups.

▶ Together, make a soup or stew that contains ingredients from all food groups.

▶ A family album is often an excellent reference for a child to see how he or she has grown and changed. As you share the photos together, talk about the characteristics of each stage. For example: How did you move around when you were one year old? What foods did you eat when you were a baby? A toddler? How did you get your food? What sounds did you make? Why? What can you do now that you couldn't do then?

✂ -

IT'S ALIVE

Family Letter Ⓑ

Dear Family,

We have begun discussing the following activity in the classroom, and hope you will enjoy completing the activity with your child.

Together, try to grow a plant without a seed. Place four toothpicks around the centre of a white or sweet potato. Place the potato into a glass of water so that the stem end of the potato is immersed in the water. Observe the potato over several days, adding water if the level becomes too low.

Copyright © 2000 Pearson Education Canada Inc.

Line Master 1

Animals

Copyright © 2000 Pearson Education Canada Inc.

It's Alive

Line Master 2

Growth and Change

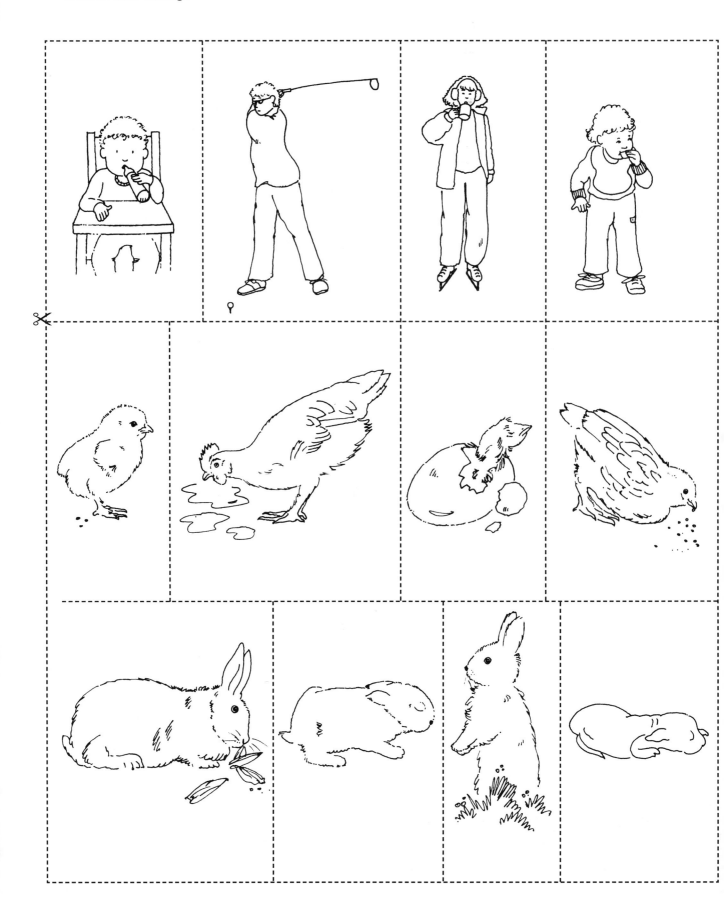

Copyright © 2000 Pearson Education Canada Inc.

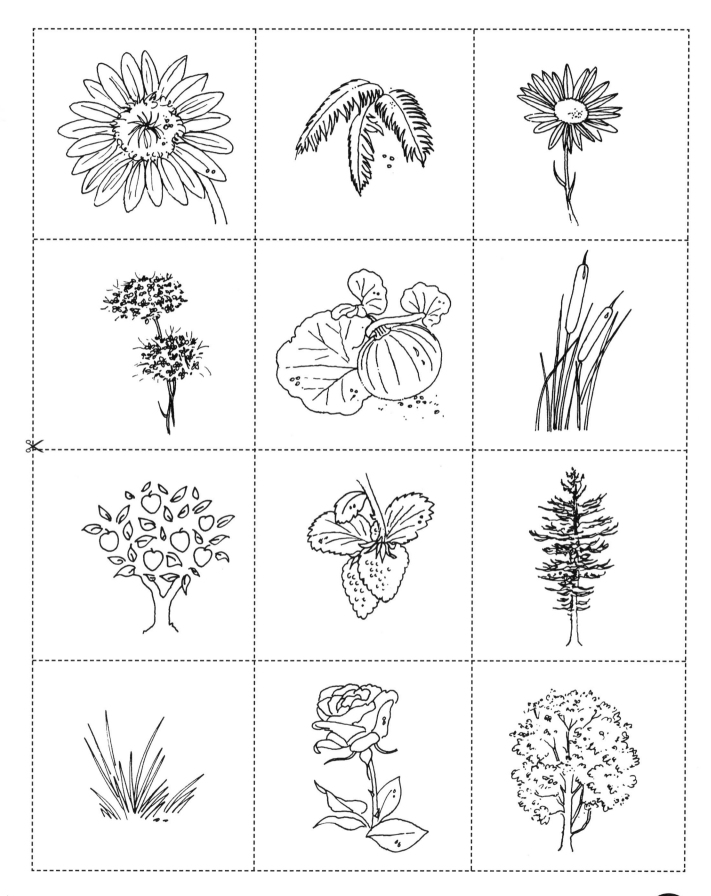

Copyright © 2000 Pearson Education Canada Inc. It's Alive

Name: _____   Date: _____

It's Alive

Draw a living thing.

Describe your living thing. *(use your words to tell about it)*

What does your living thing need?

 Copyright © 2000 Pearson Education Canada Inc.

Looking at Shoes

UNIT OVERVIEW

This unit engages children in exploring, observing, describing, and investigating the materials used to make objects. The context of shoes is used because of their familiarity, diversity, and availability as a material for children to examine. More importantly children can explore and develop an understanding that shoes are objects that are made from different materials and that these materials have specific properties.

- **Children begin by using their senses to describe** the various characteristics of an object and the materials used to make it.

- **Children learn** that shoes and other objects which are made for a specific purpose can be made from different materials. They identify and describe a variety of materials in their immediate surroundings. As they do this, children make the distinction between objects and materials and see that the objects they identify are made from materials that are important to their purpose and function. Through this exploration and discussion, children become aware that the same material can be used to make many different objects.

- **Children explore** ways of adding new materials to play dough to change its appearance, texture, and smell. Children also test different materials to determine which ones are waterproof, and communicate the procedure and results to others.

- Finally, **children make objects** by combining and modifying various materials. As they work with the materials and explore the problems of design, children begin to identify different ways materials can be joined together, demonstrate an understanding of reusing materials, and recognize that properties of materials help an object serve its function.

CONCEPT DEVELOPMENT AND OTHER ISSUES

Young children naturally use their senses to learn about the world around them. In this unit, their senses help them learn about the properties of objects and the characteristics of the materials that make up those objects. Model and encourage a wide range of vocabulary when describing and comparing objects and materials.

Invite children to explore the sorting bins, the senses containers, and the materials at the Design and Build Centre (see Activity Bank) to learn about the properties of materials.

COLLECTING MATERIALS

In two activities children design and create objects from collected and recycled materials. You will need such materials as *cardboard rolls, trays, boxes, paper bags, shoe boxes, small pieces of wood, paper and fabric scraps, plastic lids, smooth rimmed cans,* and *plastic and wooden spools,* as well as *fasteners, such as wood and regular glue, cellophane and masking tape, pipe cleaners, string, rubber bands, ribbon, yarn,* and *staplers.*

Establish a recycling area in the classroom to focus children's attention on materials, as well as on the value of recycling and reusing. Label recycling bins with the name of the material (glass) and an example of an object made with that material (jar).

Ask families to lend interesting footwear to a Shoe Interest Centre. At the centre children can examine and discuss shoes from different cultures, shoes made of different materials, and shoes that serve different purposes.

Unit Planner

ACTIVITY FOCUS ➡ CHILDREN:	TIME	MATERIALS
A LAUNCH THE TOPIC ACTIVITY		
state what they know about shoes and materials that they and other objects are made from	1 class period	chart paper, collection of shoes
B ACTIVITY BANK ACTIVITIES		
❶ **Tell About It** — describe materials using information gathered by senses		pineapple, baseball, tea bag
❷ **Wanted: One Box of Raisins!** — describe materials using information gathered by senses	Take 5	small boxes of raisins
❸ **What Made that Sound?** — describe materials using information gathered by senses		
❹ **What's in the Bag?** — describe materials using information gathered by senses		paper bag, small objects
❺ **What Is It?** — describe materials using information gathered by senses		
❻ **Penny Drop** — describe materials using information gathered by senses; demonstrate how materials can be manipulated to make different sounds		pennies, container
❼ **A Senses Walk** — describe materials using information gathered by senses; sort objects by material	Take 30	writing and colouring materials
❽ **Making Different Sounds** — demonstrate how materials can be manipulated to make different sounds		empty bottles, water, food colouring, spoon, straws, cardboard, glue
❾ **Buckle Up** — identify materials that can be used to join and fasten other materials		variety of fasteners
❿ **Sorting Bins** — sort objects and describe the materials from which they are made		objects made from different materials
⓫ **Using Your Senses** — describe materials using information gathered by senses	Take Time	containers; smell, sound, and touch items; paper towels or cotton balls
⓬ **Design and Build Centre** — design a usable product that is aesthetically pleasing		variety of materials for designing and building
⓭ **Recycling in the Classroom** — demonstrate ways of reusing materials and objects, recognize that certain materials can be recycled		paper and writing materials, several large containers
C STUDENT BOOK/FLIP CHART BOOK ACTIVITIES		
❶ **Shoes are made of different materials.** — *pages 2-3* describe materials from which objects are made	1 to 2 class periods	pencil, chart paper, marker
❷ **Shoes can be made of cloth, wood, or leather.** — *pages 4-5* use their senses to identify a variety of materials	1 to 2 class periods	similar objects made of different materials, paper bag
❸ **Sometimes we change materials to make shoes.** — *pages 6-7* describe ways in which materials can be altered	1 class period	crayons, pencils, markers, scrap paper, play dough, scented materials, textured materials, colouring agents
❹ **Shoes protect your feet.** — *pages 8-9* identify properties of materials	2 class periods	water, newspaper, eye dropper, materials to test
❺ **Shoes do up in different ways.** — *pages 10-11* explore fasteners	2 class periods	materials for building and fastening
❻ **You can use a shoe box or bag again.** — *pages 12-13* design a usable product using found materials	2 to 3 class periods	shoe boxes or bags, found materials, craft materials, scissors, tape, glue, markers
❼ **At Home** — *pages 14-15* recognize that objects made of certain materials can be recycled	equivalent to 1 class period	
❽ **Look Back** — *page 16* identify objects made of a variety of materials;	1 class period	
D DEMONSTRATE WHAT YOU KNOW TASK		
❶ design a usable product using found materials, describe materials from which objects are made	1 class period plus	

ACTIVITY DESCRIPTION CHILDREN:	LINE MASTERS	ASSESSMENT
- sort shoes in a variety of ways, identify materials that make up shoes; create a 'Know/Wonder/Learned' chart	Family Letter Master A	
- describe an object using the five senses		
- describe a box of raisins		
- identify an object by the sound it makes		
- guess the identity of a hidden object from clues		
- play I Spy using clues based on the senses		
- compare sounds made by different groups of the same materials		
- observe their environment using all five senses		observation, portfolio
- describe sounds made by piped instruments		
- survey the class about fasteners on clothing		
- guess the rule as various materials are sorted		interview
- identify pairs of objects by smell, sound, and touch		observation
- design and build objects using a variety of materials and fasteners		
- focus on recycling in the classroom		
- draw and label objects made of at least two different materials	LM 1	observation, portfolio
- sort objects by the material from which they are made		observation
- change play dough in a variety of ways and observe the changes	LM2	observation, portfolio
- experiment with materials to determine if they are waterproof	LM 3	observation, portfolio
- use fasteners to connect materials		observation, portfolio
- make something usable from a shoe box or bag		observation, interview
- with their families, discuss recycling and match items to the proper recycling bin	Family Letter Master B	
- identify shoes from clues given about materials		
- design and draw a usable object and label its materials	LM 4	rubric

PLANNING AHEAD

TEACHER RESOURCES

Richards, Roy. An Early Start to Science. London: Macdonald Educational, 1987.

BOOKS FOR CHILDREN

Cobb, Vicki. Sneakers Meet Your Feet. Boston: Little Brown, 1985.

Gibbons, Gail. Paper Paper Everywhere. San Diego: Harcourt Brace Jovanovich, 1983.

Gibbons, Gail. Recycle! Boston: Little, Brown, 1992.

Lanteigne, Helen. The Seven Chairs. Toronto: Key Porter Books, 1998.

Miller, Margaret. Whose Shoes? New York: Greenwillow, 1991.

WEB SITES

BrainPOP: www.brainpop.com

Realm of Recycling: www.bconnex.net/~mbuchana/realms/page1/recycle.html

Recycle City: www.epa.gov/recyclecity

CD-ROMS

I Love Science by DK Multimedia.Win/Mac

The Way Things Work by DK Multimedia.Win/Mac

VIDEOS

Eco Education Program, Ministry of Environment, Lands and Parks

Garbage Tale — An Environmental Adventure, B.C. Learning Commission Inc.

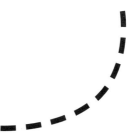

Cross-Curricular Overview

LINK TO...
SOCIAL STUDIES UNIT
PEOPLE AT WORK

Any time after Activity 6, you might wish to discuss the role of people who work in the community, the focus of the unit **People at Work** in Ginn Social Studies. Engage children in a discussion about garbage collection and recycling, and about the workers who are responsible for these jobs. Children can role-play or tell stories to demonstrate their understanding of how workers help a community.

JUG BAND

Curriculum Link: *Music*
Use any time after: Activity 2

Purpose
- Produce a specific effect using various sound sources.
- Accompany songs using appropriate instruments.
- Create and perform musical compositions.

Materials
- simple instruments as listed below
- found materials for making instruments (empty tissue boxes, elastic bands, small containers with lids, dried beans, rice, variety of sticks or wooden spoons, empty plastic jugs)

Get Started
Display a variety of simple instruments — wooden sticks, bells, maracas, drums, and so on. Ask a volunteer to choose an instrument, then demonstrate to the class how to use it. Keep going until the children have heard each instrument.
Ask:
- What did you have to do to make a sound with the (sticks)?

Explain to the children that they will be using found materials to create instruments, then creating a class band. Show the children the materials and ask:
- What sound would you like to make? What materials do you think you will need to make an instrument that makes that sound? What sound can you make using something plastic? Metal? Rubber?

Work On It
Invite the children to choose their materials, and give them time to create their instruments. As they work, they can test their instruments to see if they are able to create sound, and revise them if necessary.

Communicate
Children can demonstrate their instruments to the class. Ask:
- What materials are part of your instrument? Does the material have something do with the sound it makes?

Divide the class into groups, or work as a large group, and have the children play their instruments together. They can follow a recording of a familiar song, sing a familiar song and play along with it, or simply to enjoy the music they can make together.

WHERE DOES THIS GO

Curriculum Link: *Mathematics*
Use any time after: Activity 2

Purpose
- Compare, sort, and classify concrete objects.

Get Started
Begin by drawing attention to the children's shoes. Ask:
- What do you notice about the shoes you are wearing? Who is wearing running shoes?

Invite children wearing running shoes to stand together, and ask:
- What is the same about the shoes these children are wearing? How are the running shoes the same? How are they different?

Then ask:
- What other type of shoes are children wearing? Guide children in forming another group based on the footwear several are wearing. Discuss how these shoes are the same and how they are different. Explain to the children that they have just sorted themselves by the type of shoes they are wearing.

Work On It
Repeat by having children identify other attributes or features of their shoes such as colour, type of fastener, materials, print, texture of soles, and so on. List the different ways children sort the shoes and add to it throughout the unit.

Communicate
After sorting and resorting their shoes, ask:
- What did we find out about the different shoes you wear to school? What are some sorting rules we used? Were you ever in two groups at the same time? Why?

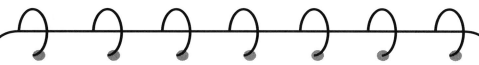

FOUND OBJECTS SCULPTURE

Curriculum Link: *Visual Arts*
Use anytime after: Activity 6

Purpose:
- Make artistic choices in their work, using at least one of the elements of design specified for this grade.
- Produce three-dimensional works of art that communicate thoughts and feelings.

Materials:
- picture of any kind of sculpture
- variety of found objects
- variety of fasteners
- craft materials as necessary

Get Started
Show children a picture of a sculpture. Explain that it is a sculpture and ask:
- What is the artist showing with this sculpture? Why do you think the artist decided to make a sculpture instead of another type of art work? Why was a sculpture a good choice?

Tell the children that they are going to make a sculpture using found objects of their choice.

Work On It
Invite the children to brainstorm things they think they could portray in a sculpture, and record their responses. Then provide them with a variety of found materials, such as cardboard rolls, fruit baskets, foam trays, buttons, spools, film canisters, and so on. Invite them to choose an idea from the list or to decide on something else they would like to build using their found materials, to gather the materials they need, and to create their sculpture.

Communicate
When children have completed their art works, invite them to share their work with the class. Encourage them to describe what they made and what materials they chose. Display children's completed work in the classroom.

A LAUNCH THE TOPIC

Have children sit around a large collection of shoes and other footwear. Begin by asking the children to imagine that these shoes were in a shoe store and it is their job to organize and promote them. Take some time to talk about the shoes in the collection, focusing on the purpose, origin, parts, and materials of the shoes children select to discuss. Ask:

■ How might we sort these shoes to display them in our shoe store?

Invite volunteers to suggest ways to sort the shoes and have children help place the shoes into appropriate groups. Discuss how the shoes in each group are alike and different. Create labels for each group and continue to sort and resort the shoes.

Explain to the children that they will be talking about the materials from which shoes and other objects are made and that the collection of shoes will be available for them to examine. Encourage children to bring in other examples of footwear to add to the collection. If possible, add measuring tools, magnifying lenses, recording materials, and books and resources about shoes and materials to the Shoe Interest Centre. Some children might be interested in creating posters that show the characteristics, materials, and features of a particular shoe. Post these around the interest centre or on a bulletin board.

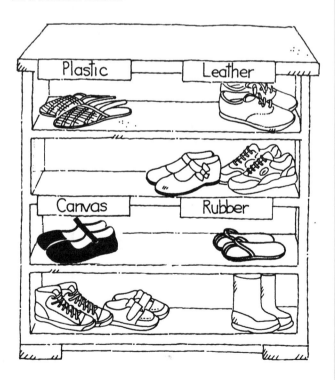

KEEP IT GOING

After children have had an opportunity to explore and discuss the collection of shoes begin to focus their attention on particular materials that are used to make the shoes. Post charts with headings describing different materials children identify on the shoes such as rubber, plastic, metal, cloth, and wood. Read the labels and have children identify other objects that are made of the same material. As each item is added to the list, ask:

■ What is the (table) used for? Why is (wood) a good material for a table? What other materials could a (table) be made from?

Children can add to the list over time. As a class, read the list from time to time, discussing the items listed.

As you begin this unit, send home Family Letter A. Encourage families to do some of the activities suggested to enhance children's learning about family and friends.

B ACTIVITY BANK

1 TELL ABOUT IT

PURPOSE: – Describe various materials using information gathered by using their senses.

MATERIALS: pineapple
new baseball
tea bag
other items that can be described using all the senses

Pass an object around the circle, and ask the children to use their senses to tell something about it. You might prompt observations by asking:

■ What words describe how it feels? Tell us about what you see.

Record the children's observations. Select a different object each time the activity is repeated.

2 WANTED: ONE BOX OF RAISINS!

PURPOSE: – Describe various materials using information gathered by using their senses.

MATERIALS: small boxes of raisins

Provide pairs or small groups with a small box of raisins. Ask the children to use their senses to describe the box and the raisins. Record their descriptions.

3 WHAT MADE THAT SOUND?

PURPOSE: – Describe various materials using information gathered by using their senses.

Ask the children to close their eyes. Make a sound for the children to identify and describe, for example, drop a penny on the table, tap the window, turn on the tap, move a chair across the floor, write on the chalkboard, or tap two pencils together.

4 WHAT'S IN THE BAG?

PURPOSE: – Describe various materials using information gathered by using their senses.

MATERIALS: paper bag
small objects

Place an object (block, eraser, table tennis ball, elastic band) into the paper bag without letting children see. Invite a volunteer to put his or her hand in the bag and describe the object. Challenge the volunteer — or the rest of the class — to guess what the object is.

5 WHAT IS IT?

PURPOSE: – Describe various materials using information gathered by using their senses.

Describe an object in the classroom by giving sensory clues, for example, "I am thinking about something that is round and made of glass and metal. It makes a quiet clicking sound every time a moving part goes past a number. If you touched it, it would feel hard and smooth. What is it?" (clock)

6 PENNY DROP

PURPOSE: – Describe various materials using information gathered by using their senses.

– Demonstrate ways materials can be manipulated to make different sounds.

MATERIALS: pennies
container

Ask the children to close their eyes and use their sense of hearing to count how many pennies are dropped into a container. Repeat by dropping pennies into a second container. Then shake each container and have the children compare and describe the sounds they make.

7) A SENSES WALK

PURPOSE:
- Describe various materials using information gathered by using their senses.
- Sort objects and describe the different materials from which those objects are made.

MATERIALS: writing and colouring materials

Take the children to locations in the school where they can observe many sights and sounds, for example, the library, the office, or the playground. Invite children to use their senses to describe what they see, hear, smell, and feel. Ask them to describe the different materials used to make things in those locations. Record their descriptions.

When the children return to the classroom, they can illustrate some of their observations. Challenge children to sort the pictures by location or by sense.

8) MAKING DIFFERENT SOUNDS

PURPOSE:
- Demonstrate ways in which various materials can be manipulated to produce different sounds and describe their findings.

MATERIALS:
empty bottles
water
food colouring
spoon
straws
cardboard
glue

Create a bottle xylophone by filling several bottles with increasing amounts of coloured water. Tap each bottle in turn with a spoon and ask the children to describe the sounds they hear. The more water there is in the bottle, the higher the sound.

Invite the children to create their own piped instrument by seriating straws from longest to shortest and gluing them between two strips of cardboard. Encourage the children to explore and describe the sounds they can make by pointing the straws downward and blowing across the top of them. The shorter the straw, the higher the sound.

9) BUCKLE UP

PURPOSE:
- Identify materials that can be used to join and fasten other materials.

MATERIALS:
variety of fasteners (shoelace, safety pin, zipper, button, thread, ribbon, snaps, barrette, buckle, elastic)

Explain to the children that many different materials can be used to join and fasten other materials. Show each fastener and ask:

■ What is this? What would it hold together? How would it be used? What materials were used to make it?

Conduct a survey to find out how many children can find each fastener on their clothing. Invite children to examine what they are wearing, and record their results using your list. Interpret the results of the survey. Consider repeating the same survey over the next few days. How are the results the same? How are they different?

Invite the children to bring in other examples of fasteners to share with the class.

10) SORTING BINS

PURPOSE:
- Sort objects and describe the different materials from which those objects are made.

MATERIALS:
objects made from different materials (wood, plastic, metal, paper)

Present a collection of classroom and found objects that are made from plastic, wood, paper, and metal. Begin separating a number of items into a set (wood) and ask:

■ What's my rule for sorting?

If necessary, add a few more items to the set. Ask the children to describe the similarities and differences of the objects in the set. Challenge them to find other classroom items to place in the set.

Repeat the activity, sorting the items into two or more groups (plastic and paper).

You may wish to place the collections of materials in bins and use them as an ongoing activity throughout the unit. As children sort the collections, they can explain their sorting rules. Challenge them to re-sort the materials in many different ways.

11 USING YOUR SENSES

PURPOSE: – Describe various materials using information gathered by using their senses.

MATERIALS: containers
smell, sound and touch items as indicated
paper towels or cotton balls

Prepare five pairs of smelling containers by placing objects with distinctive smells (garlic, perfume, almond extract, coffee, flavoured toothpaste, onion, and so on) on paper or cotton in the containers. Be aware of any food allergies that may be triggered by the smelling containers.

Prepare five pairs of sound containers by placing objects which make distinctive sounds when shaken (rice, pennies, a block, a bell, paper clips) into sealed plastic containers.

Prepare five pairs of feeling containers by placing objects with distinctive textures (sandpaper, a piece of silk, a smooth rock, gummy worms) into empty tissue boxes.

Invite the children to select one set of containers and use the appropriate sense to match each pair. Encourage children to describe their observations and explain their findings as they work.

12 DESIGN AND BUILD CENTRE

PURPOSE: – Design a usable product that is aesthetically pleasing and construct it by combining and modifying materials that they have selected themselves.

MATERIALS: variety of materials for designing and building

Establish a Design and Build Centre which children can visit over the course of this unit. Provide paper, rulers, drawing tools, and junk material such as boxes, cylinders, cardboard trays, paper bags, wood scraps, and so on. Include materials for fastening and decorating as well. Encourage children to plan what they would like to make before they build it.

13 RECYCLING IN THE CLASSROOM

PURPOSE: – Demonstrate ways of reusing materials and objects in daily activities; recognize that objects made of certain materials can be recycled.

MATERIALS: paper and writing materials
several large containers

Establish a recycling program in your classroom. Invite the children to create signs to post over the various recycling containers and the garbage pail to help others know where to put their waste. Visit the school's recycling centre so the children can see and discuss the school's efforts to recycle and reuse.

SUSTAINABLE DEVELOPMENT

Why do we reuse things?
Why is reusing helpful?

Student Book pages 2–3

" Shoes are made of different materials. "

PURPOSE:

– Identify each of the senses.

– Describe various materials using information gathered by using their senses.

– Sort objects and describe the different materials from which those objects are made.

– Identify properties of materials that are important to the purpose and function of the objects that are made from them.

MATERIALS:

• pencil
• chart paper
• marker
• copy of LM 1 for each child

TIME:

1 to 2 class periods

SKILL FOCUS:

observing, inferring

GET STARTED

Give each child a pencil. Ask:

■ What can you tell us about your pencil? What does it look like? How does it feel? Which senses have you used to tell about the pencil so far? What other senses can you use? What do you use it for? What materials do you see? Tell about the wood (lead, metal, rubber).

On chart paper record the children's descriptions. Choose one of the list words and challenge children to find other things in the room that are the same in that way. (What else can you find that is made of wood? Is red? Is hard?)

WORK ON IT

USING PAGES 2 AND 3

Encourage children to look closely at the shoe on the page and to compare it to their own. Discuss the different materials in the shoe, reading the labels together. Children can look for similar materials in their own shoes.

Discuss why different materials are used for different parts of the shoe.

Display a pencil with an eraser. Sketch it on the chalkboard, and with the children's help, label its different materials. Discuss whether any of the materials used to make a pencil were also used to make the shoe in the book.

BEYOND THE PAGE

Provide children with a copy of LM 1. Together read the words that form the border. Ask children to choose a classroom object that is made of at least two different materials, to draw it on the page, and label their drawing. They can use the words on the border and the shoe labels in their book for reference.

COMMUNICATE

Challenge children to describe their drawing using only the labels and not showing the picture. For example: My object is made of wax. It is wrapped in paper. What is it? (crayon)

After children have guessed the answer, ask questions to address how and why materials are used. Ask:

■ What do you use a (crayon) for? Why is it made of wax? (makes a mark, has colour) What does the paper do? (protects the crayon, protects your hands)

ASSESSMENT OPPORTUNITY

Reflect on how the children participated during the discussion and the type of descriptive vocabulary they used. Can they identify and draw an object from their environment that is made of at least two materials? Are they able to label the materials used to manufacture the object? The finished recording can be placed in the child's **portfolio**.

" Shoes can be made of cloth, wood, or leather. "

PURPOSE:

- Describe materials using information gathered by using their senses.
- Sort objects and describe the different materials from which they are made.
- Compare objects constructed for similar purposes and identify the similarities and differences between their corresponding parts and their materials.
- Demonstrate ways in which materials can be manipulated to produce different sounds.
- Identify, through observation, the same material in different objects.
- Identify materials commonly used in manufactured objects as well as the source of those materials.

MATERIALS:

- three blocks made of different materials (wood, plastic, sponge)
- paper bag
- small objects of different materials (plastic and wooden blocks, metal paper clips, glass marbles, small paper squares)

TIME:

1 to 2 class periods

SKILL FOCUS

observing, comparing, interpreting

GET STARTED

Display three blocks made of different materials. Ask children to describe them using their sense of sight and then, after passing the blocks around, their sense of touch. Record their descriptions.

Have children try to identify the blocks by using other senses. For example, drop blocks on different surfaces and challenge children to guess what kind of block they hear, or invite children to close their eyes and smell each block to identify it.

WORK ON IT

USING PAGES 4 AND 5

Have children look at the page and identify what each shoe is made of. Ask them to find a shoe on the page that is most like their own, then tell how the shoes are the same and how they are different. Invite children to compare the pictured shoes by asking:

- How are all of the shoes the same? Different? Why are there so many different kinds? Which shoe would you buy to wear to a party? To wear every day? Which shoe looks the most comfortable? Why? Uncomfortable? Why? Why do you suppose most shoes arc not made of wood? Glass?

Focus children's attention on the cotton plant, the tree, and the cow. Ask:

- What material do you get from each of these sources? What shoes on the page are made from each of these materials? What shoes on the page are made from other materials? What materials are they made of?

BEYOND THE PAGE

Fill the paper bag with small objects of different materials. Divide the children into pairs or small groups. Invite one member from each group to choose an object from the bag. Challenge each group to find things in the classroom that are made of the same material as the object they chose, and make a recording of them.

COMMUNICATE

Invite a volunteer from each group to present the group's findings to the class. Discuss children's observations by asking:

- What are many things in the classroom made of? How would you describe the (metal/plastic/ glass/paper) things you found? How are they alike? Different? What material isn't used much to make the things that we have in our classroom? What is the window made of? Could it be made of wood? Why not?

EXTENSION

Talk about the source of wood and paper (children likely know that these are products of trees). Draw and post an outline of a large tree. Encourage children to make drawings or cut out magazine pictures of different things that come from trees and glue them to the tree.

ASSESSMENT OPPORTUNITY

This activity has children use their senses to examine objects and describe the properties of the materials. Is the child able to identify the different materials of which blocks and shoes are made? What word does the child use to describe the properties of a material? Is the child able to identify objects in his or her immediate environment that are made with a specific type of material? Record your responses and **observations** on AM 1, AM 2, or AM 3.

SUSTAINABLE DEVELOPMENT

How can we take care of our shoes so they last longer?

" Sometimes we change materials to make shoes. "

PURPOSE:

- Describe, using their observations, ways in which materials can be changed to alter their appearance.
- Describe materials using information gathered by using their senses.
- Plan investigations to answer questions or solve problems.
- Record relevant observations and findings.
- Communicate the procedures and results of investigations.
- Use appropriate vocabulary.

MATERIALS:

- crayons, pencils, markers
- scrap paper
- play dough
- scented materials (almond or vanilla extract, cinnamon, perfume)
- textured materials (rice, sand, gravel)
- colouring agents (food colouring, juice powder, paint powder)
- LM 2 for each child

TIME:

1 class period

PLAY IT SAFE:

Be aware of food and other allergies. Extremely allergic children may react to smell.

SKILL FOCUS:

observing, comparing, communicating

GET STARTED

Show children a set of crayons and invite them to describe the similarities and differences within the set. Do the same with sets of pencils and markers. Then invite children to describe the similarities and differences between the three sets. Ask:

- What materials are they made of? What do we use them for? What kind of marks do they make?

Encourage children to use their senses to observe and describe the materials. Give children scrap paper and challenge them to change the appearance of the paper in some way. Have children show their scrap of paper and tell how the appearance changed and what they did to change it.

WORK ON IT

USING PAGES 6 AND 7

Divide the class into small groups and give each some play dough to explore. After children have explored and described the play dough, have them look at pages 6 and 7 to find out how they can change its appearance, smell, and texture. Review the materials by asking:

- What materials do we need? What will you use to change the colour? What can you add to the play dough to change the smell? The texture?

BEYOND THE PAGE

Set up the materials for changing appearance, smell, and texture at three centres, and set up a centre where children can make models with play dough. Invite children to rotate through these areas. Provide each group with the necessary materials and with copies of LM 2 for recording.

COMMUNICATE

Have volunteers discuss the changes they made by asking:

- How did you change the look of the play dough? The smell? The texture?

Ask children to suggest other materials they could use to change the play dough. Together make a plan for collecting the materials and encourage children to continue their investigation on other days with a new supply of play dough. Children can leave the play dough to harden, then consider how it has changed.

ASSESSMENT OPPORTUNITY

Here is an opportunity to **observe** how children conduct a test to change a material and communicate the results of their actions. Are children able to change the play dough in different ways and describe the changes? Do children use their senses and appropriate vocabulary in their descriptions? Do they ask other questions or suggest other ways to change the play dough? Record your observations on AM 3. The completed LM 2 can be placed in the children's **portfolio**.

" Shoes protect your feet. "

PURPOSE:

- Identify properties of materials important to the purpose and function of the objects made from them.

- Ask questions about and identify needs and problems related to objects and materials.

- Plan investigations to respond.

- Record relevant findings.

- Use appropriate vocabulary in describing their investigations

- Communicate the procedures and results of investigations.

MATERIALS:

- water
- newspaper
- eye dropper
- materials for testing (paper towel, tin foil, cardboard, plastic wrap, cloth swatches, felt pieces, plastic bags, paper bags, coloured cellophane, foam plates)
- copy of LM 3 or sorting mat for each group

TIME:

2 class periods

SKILL FOCUS:

predicting, experimenting, communicating

GET STARTED

Engage children in a discussion about how materials are used to keep them dry, warm, and cool. Ask:

- What do you wear on a cold day? On a warm day? Are they made of the same materials? What do you wear on a rainy day? Why does it keep you dry? What are other ways to keep things dry? What are things that keep you dry made of?

WORK ON IT

USING PAGES 8 AND 9

Have children look at the pages. Ask:

- How do the thongs keep your feet cool? What material are they made of? How do the mukluks keep your feet warm? What material are they made of? Which shoes would you wear when you know your feet might get wet? Why? What are those shoes made of?

Explain to the children that they will be testing materials to learn more about them. Give each group a set of materials, and discuss which materials would keep something dry.

Once children have made their predictions explain that scientists always have a plan, based on a prediction, before they carry out a test or an experiment. Review the steps that children will take by asking:

- What materials do you need to do the test? What will you do first? Second? After that? How will you keep track of what you discover?

BEYOND THE PAGE

Give children time to test their materials. They can write, draw, or tell about what they discovered. They can use LM 3 to show how they sorted the materials.

COMMUNICATE

Meet to discuss the observations children made. Ask:

- What did you find out? Which materials are waterproof? Which ones are not? What questions do you have about the materials? What other materials would you like to test?

Provide time for children to investigate other questions they pose about materials (for example a child may wish to choose an object and make something to keep it dry.)

ASSESSMENT OPPORTUNITY

Watch to find out which materials children predict will be waterproof and how they conduct the test to find out. How do children keep track of what they find out? How do they describe their investigations and findings? Do they suggest other materials they would like to test or other questions they would like to pursue? Place children's recordings in their **portfolios**, and use AM 4 to track the portfolio entries.

PURPOSE:

– Sort objects and describe the different materials from which those objects are made.

– Identify properties of materials important to the purpose and function of the objects made from them.

– Identify materials that can be used to join and fasten other materials.

MATERIALS:

• materials for building (small pieces of wood, fabric swatches, paper scraps, plastic lids, small tin cans, empty paper towel and toilet paper rolls, discarded plastic and wooden spools) and fastening (cellophane and masking tape, stapler, wood glue, regular glue, darning needle and yarn, elastic bands)

TIME:

2 class periods

SKILL FOCUS:

classifying, interpreting, making models

" Shoes do up in different ways. "

GET STARTED

Encourage children to examine their clothing for fasteners. Continue to explore how things are fastened by having children look around the room for things that are attached and how they are attached. Show how hinges are used to attach the door to the frame. Show how windows move and are fastened to the frame. Continue to search the room.

WORK ON IT

USING PAGES 10 AND 11

Ask children to think about how their shoes fasten. Ask:

■ Which shoes on these pages fasten like your own? What type of fasteners do you prefer on shoes? Why? Which of the fasteners on this page are made of metal? Plastic? Attached with thread? Encourage children to explain how their favourite fasteners work.

(You might wish to explain that Velcro was inspired by nature. A Swiss engineer got the idea for this woven, plastic hooks-and-loops fastener in 1948 when he looked under a microscope at how plant burrs were stuck to his socks.)

Ask each child to remove one shoe, then challenge the group to sort the shoes into groups according to how they fasten. Compare the number of shoes in each group. Ask:

■ How do most of the shoes in our class fasten? How many more (lace-up) shoes are there than (slip-on) shoes? Do you think that we would find the same type of fasteners on shoes in other classrooms?

BEYOND THE PAGE

Explain to the children that fasteners aren't only used to do up shoes and clothes. Things such as glue, tape, staples, and so on are also fasteners.

Provide children with building and fastening materials. Challenge them to think about how they could use the two together by giving examples.

Challenge children to choose at least three materials, then to build a structure and fasten it together.

COMMUNICATE

Invite them to share their structure and to explain why they selected certain materials and fasteners.

EXTENSION

Invite children to change the appearance of their structure by decorating it. Discuss together how they might change the materials to make their structure waterproof, a different colour, and so on.

ASSESSMENT OPPORTUNITY

Observe how well children combine and modify materials to make their structure. Are they able to use appropriate materials to combine and fasten other materials? Are they able to explain their choice of materials and their building decisions and actions in a clear way? Some children might want to draw or write about their object. Place this record in their **portfolio**.

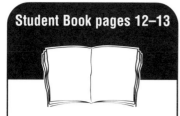
"You can use a shoe box or bag again."

PURPOSE:

– Design a usable product that is aesthetically pleasing and construct it by combining and modifying materials that they have selected themselves.

– Demonstrate ways of reusing materials and objects in daily activities.

– Communicate the procedures and results of investigations.

MATERIALS:

• shoe boxes or shoe bags
• a rich collection of found and craft materials (cardboard rolls, small boxes, tissue paper, string, pipe cleaners)
• scissors
• tape
• glue
• markers

TIME:

2 to 3 class periods

SKILL FOCUS:

making models, communicating

GET STARTED

Engage children in a discussion about using materials to make something. Then discuss that the materials in worn-out or used-up objects may still be able to be used to make something else. Ask:

• What can you find in the classroom that was made using recycled materials? (tin cans for holding pencils or paints, boxes cut down for holding paper) Have you ever used cans, paper rolls, or anything like them to make something? What did you make?

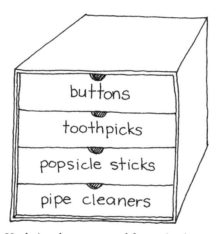

Used pizza boxes are good for storing items.

WORK ON IT

USING PAGES 12 AND 13

Encourage children to describe the materials used to make the items on the page. Ask:

• Which objects were made using a shoe box? A bag? Which object was made using paper? Wood? Which was made using more than one type of material? Which do you think was easy to make? Most difficult? Why?

Explain to children that they will design and build something that they can use. Say:

• You see some useful things that were made by reusing materials. What can you make? What will you use it for?

Ask children to consider what materials are available and what else they might need. Discuss different ways to attach materials and different ways to enhance the appearance of their work.

BEYOND THE PAGE

Provide children with the necessary materials and invite them to create something.

COMMUNICATE

When they are finished, they can present their creations. Encourage children to explain the challenges they faced and how they overcame them. Encourage them to tell how they would build the object differently next time and which additional materials they wished they had.

EXTENSION

Children can create advertisements or commercials for their creations to describe the materials they used and why their item is useful.

Arrange a class visit to a place such as a bakery, a factory, or a garage, where children can see things being created from materials.

ASSESSMENT OPPORTUNITY

Observe as children select materials, solve building problems, and attach and combine materials. Are children able to describe the function of their object and identify the properties of the materials they used? How do children approach the task and the materials? Record your observations on AM 3.

SUSTAINABLE DEVELOPMENT

Why is it good to reuse things? How does reusing help our environment?

PURPOSE:

– Recognize that objects made of certain materials can be recycled.

– Communicate with home.

MATERIALS:

• Family Letter B (optional)

TIME:

1 class period

SKILL FOCUS:

observing, comparing

At Home

GET STARTED

Have the children look at materials collected for recycling in your classroom, the school office, or the lunchroom. Focus children's attention on the fact that recycling these materials keeps them out of landfill sites. Help them to think about the amount of material that one class could collect in a month, how much all the classes in the school could collect in a month, and then how much the school could collect in one year.

Discuss with the children the importance of reusing, rather than throwing out, all that material.

WORK ON IT

USING PAGES 14 AND 15

Together, read pages 14 and 15. Children might be interested to know that the rubber from old running shoes can be recycled. It is ground up with other kinds of recycled rubber, then used as a cushioned base mat for a certain kind of gymnasium floor, as shown on the page. The mat is topped with two coats of

urethane. Markings are painted on the floor when the urethane is dry.

Have children look at the task on the page. Send home the Student Book or Family Letter B for children and their families to sort the materials together. If you prefer, continue the activity in the classroom. Have children work in small groups. Assign each group one of the containers on the page and have each list all the items that belong in that container.

COMMUNICATE

Continue to engage children in discussion about recycling. Questions like the following can promote the sharing of ideas:

- What materials do you recycle at home? Where have you seen recycling bins? How could we reuse some of the paper in our classroom? How might we recycle some of our empty containers? What kind of recycling happens in the lunchroom? What recycling of materials happens in the school office?

PURPOSE:

– Describe various materials using information gathered by using their senses.

– Identify the same material in different objects.

SKILL FOCUS:

observing

Look Back

WORK ON IT

USING PAGE 16

Together, read page 16 in the Student Book and ensure that everyone understands the task. Have children complete the activity on the page. Remind them to use the clues to help them find the shoes that are made of the same material as the items shown.

ANSWERS

The children will find

- terrycloth slipper (page 5)
- red patent shoe (page 11)
- Japanese or Dutch wooden shoe (pages 10-11)

COMMUNICATE

Invite children to share what they found, and to talk about what they learned about the various materials that make up the things around them.

ASSESSMENT OPPORTUNITY

Provide children with a copy of AM 5 for self-assessment. Discuss children's answers with them individually, and store completed Assessment Masters in children's portfolios.

Demonstrate What You Know

PURPOSE:

– Assess children's learning.

MATERIALS:

• juice containers made of various materials (plastic, glass, cardboard, tin, waxed cardboard)
• LM 4

SKILL FOCUS:

observing, comparing, classifying

GET STARTED

Using a collection of juice containers (plastic jug, glass bottle, cardboard box, tin can, waxed carton) focus children's attention on the different materials used for the packaging. Ask:

■ What different materials can be used to hold the juice? Why did the manufacturer use (plastic) to make the container? What can you tell us about the (plastic)? How does it feel? Smell? What sound does it make when you tap it?

Once children have identified and described each container and the material used to make it, select two to compare. Ask:

■ How are the two containers alike? How are they different? Why might someone choose to buy juice in a plastic container instead of a glass one?

ASSIGN THE TASK

Provide children with drawing and writing materials and a copy of LM 4. Explain to children how to complete each section. You might wish to brainstorm ideas as a whole class to make sure that all children understand the instructions. Children can use pages 2 and 3 in the Student Book as a model for labelling the materials in their design.

Take a look at children's work, conduct interviews, and record observations. Questions like these might prompt more detail:

■ Tell me about the object you designed. What is it used for? What materials would you use to make it? Why?

ASSESS THE TASK

The following rubric will help you assess each child's learning about materials and objects.

Performance Task Rubric	
Rubric	**Criteria**
Level 4	• child draws a detailed design for a useable object • child selects and labels appropriate materials • child describes the function of the object and properties of the materials identified
Level 3	• child draws a design for a useable object • child needs assistance to select and label appropriate materials • child describes the function of the object and some properties of the materials identified
Level 2	• child needs assistance to draw a design • child needs a great deal of assistance to select and label appropriate materials • child describes the function of the object and one property of the materials identified, with assistance
Level 1	• child has difficulty thinking of a useable object and completing a design • child does not select appropriate materials • child cannot describe the function of the object or the properties of any materials identified

LOOKING AT SHOES

Dear Family,

We are learning about how our senses help us identify materials and objects. We will be looking at what materials things are made of and comparing how materials are used. We will even be designing and making things ourselves.

Here are some activities that you can do at home to extend and reinforce our science curriculum. I hope that you enjoy them!

▶ Involve your child when you cook. Look at the ingredients together. Describe them using your senses. Then look how things change as ingredients are mixed, cooked, or baked. Describe the final product using your senses. How have things changed?

▶ Play "I Spy" using descriptions based on the senses. For example: I spy something that feels hard and smooth. It is red and a bit yellow. It tastes sweet and juicy. It doesn't make a sound when I shake it. It smells fresh and delicious. (apple)

▶ When you walk with your child, ask: What sounds do you hear? What things can you smell? What can you see that is green (any other descriptive word)?

▶ Put together a group of objects made of the same material. For example, find four to six things made of plastic. Ask your child how all of the things are the same. Invite your child to find other things made of plastic.

✂ -

LOOKING AT SHOES

Family Letter B

Dear Family,

We have begun discussing the following activity in the classroom, and hope you will enjoy completing the activity with your child.

Gather a collection of recyclable materials — fine paper, newspaper, glass, plastic, and tin. Challenge your child to sort the recyclables by material, telling you what each is made of. Invite your child to draw or write about how he or she sorted.

 Copyright © 2000 Pearson Education Canada Inc.

Name: _____   Date: _____

Describing a _____

Draw an object.
Label the materials.

cloth

leather

metal

glass

paper

rubber

wood

Name: _____ Date: _____

Making Changes

Draw or write how you changed the play dough.

I. I added	Now the play dough looks
It changed the	
2. I added	Now the play dough smells
It changed the	
3. I added	Now the play dough feels
It changed the	

 Copyright © 2000 Pearson Education Canada Inc.

Name: _____   Date: _____

Testing Materials

Keeps It Dry	Doesn't Keep It Dry

Copyright © 2000 Pearson Education Canada Inc.   Looking at Shoes

Name: _____   Date: _____

Materials and Objects

Design something that you could use.

Label the materials you would use to make it.

What would you use it for?

_____

_____

_____

Looking at Shoes   Copyright © 2000 Pearson Education Canada Inc.

At the Playground

UNIT OVERVIEW

This unit engages children in observing, comparing, and creating structures. The playground showcases interesting shapes and patterns, and is a place where young children can explore and develop an understanding of the function of various structures as they climb, slide, swing, and move in many ways.

- **Children begin by identifying** a variety of structures in their immediate surroundings. They identify different shapes in these structures and see how shapes combine to form patterns. Seeing the patterns allows children to look for a new range of similarities among structures they observe.

- **Children then use familiar materials** to build their own structures. First they build structures for a classroom model of a playground. This experience is extended later when they meet the challenge of building a model of a structure with a moving part.

- Through such an experience they begin to **develop an understanding** of how parts may be connected in a system.

CONCEPT DEVELOPMENT AND OTHER ISSUES

Young children are natural builders and have engaged in building long before they entered school. As they build they develop a sense of stability, balance, and design. They learn that some solid objects stack well, while others slide, and still others can stack and slide. They have seen that wide structures are more stable than tall, skinny ones and that some materials are sturdier than others.

Children will continue to discover a great deal on their own when given time to explore a wide range of building materials. Some blocks and materials lead children naturally to building structures that are solid shapes. Providing straws, craft sticks, and toothpicks allows children to explore building frame structures. Varying the materials and allowing time for free exploration is important as most children want to satisfy their own curiosity and try out ideas with the materials before they are directed to use them for a specific task.

COLLECTING MATERIALS

This unit includes two activities in which children build model structures. Both require a variety of found materials (*blocks, empty tin cans, paper towel rolls, small cartons, paper cups, foam trays, fruit baskets, wooden or plastic spools, empty cardboard boxes*) that may not already be in the classroom. Begin a collection of these materials, then send notes home with children requesting that families send in materials appropriate for building. Have children sort the things they bring in by type so that the materials they want are easy to find and inviting to use.

You may also wish to set up a Carpentry Centre for which you will need *pieces of wood of various sizes, nails, safety glasses, hammers* and *other tools*. Post rules at the centre and remind children to read them each time they work there.

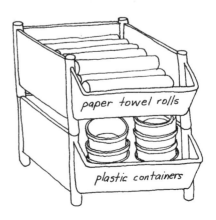

paper towel rolls

plastic containers

Unit Planner

ACTIVITY FOCUS ► CHILDREN:	TIME	MATERIALS
A) LAUNCH THE TOPIC ACTIVITY ▌▌		
state what they know about structures and how to build them; create questions for inquiry and investigation	1 class period	building materials
B) ACTIVITY BANK ACTIVITIES ▌▌		
1 Same and Different — compare form and function of structures	⬆ **Take 5** 🕐	2 objects for comparing
2 Shapes Are Everywhere — identify geometric shapes		
3 What Happens? — identify input and output of systems		
4 What Is this For? — recognize products are manufactured to meet needs		simple tool, such as a pencil
5 What Is It? — identify structures whose function is indicated by their shape	⬇	objects whose shape defines their function
6 Structure Walk — classify structures in their environment according to function	⬆ **Take 30** 🕐	
7 Pull that Pulley — describe how parts of some systems work together		pulleys, spools, paper clips, string, scissors, coat hangers
8 Make the Job Easier — select appropriate tools and utensils		small cups, cereal, variety of tools
9 Nature's Structures — distinguish between human-made structures and devices and those found in nature	⬇	natural structure, measuring tools, magnifying lenses
10 We Can Fix It! — use tools appropriately when joining materials	⬆ **Take Time** 🕐	variety of fasteners
11 Carpenters at Work — design and make structures; select appropriate tools and use them to fasten; use finishing techniques		carpentry materials
12 Architects at Work — design and make structures; use appropriate vocabulary to describe them		variety of building materials
13 How Do those Machines Work? — describe how the parts of some systems work together	⬇	collection of simple machines, functional and broken
C) STUDENT BOOK/FLIP CHART BOOK ACTIVITIES ▌▌		
1 Things we build are called structures. — *pages 2-3* identify and examine structures	1 class period	building materials from school and home, connecting blocks, wooden blocks, chart paper
2 Build a structure for a model playground. — *pages 4-5* explain the function of various structures	1 class period	paper, drawing materials, materials for skeletal structures, solid structures, finishing, and decorating
3 You can see shapes in structures. Sometimes shapes make a pattern. — *pages 6-7* identify geometric shapes and patterns in structures	1 class period	multiple sets of shape cutouts, paper, drawing materials, glue, long strips of paper, small boxes
4 Structures that do the same thing can look different. — *pages 8-9* identify similarities and differences in structures	1 class period	drawing materials, paper, building materials, toys
5 Some structures have parts that move. — *pages 10-11* identify and explore objects with moving parts	2 class periods	objects with moving parts, building materials
6 Many structures at the fair move. You can turn them on and off. — *pages 12-13* identify action required to operate a system, describe how parts of systems work together	1 class period	drawing materials, paper
7 At Home — *pages 14-15* design and make a structure using concrete materials	equivalent to 1 class period	toothpicks, modelling clay
8 Look Back — *page 16* reflect on and synthesize what they know	1 class period	
D) DEMONSTRATE WHAT YOU KNOW TASK ▌▌		
1 identify functions of different structures	1 class period plus	building materials, drawing or writing materials, scissors

Activity Description ➤ Children:	Line Masters	Assessment
- explore building materials	Family Letter Master A	
- tell about similarities and differences in objects		
- play I Spy using shapes as clues		
- describe the response to an action		
- explain the function of various items		
- identify objects by their shape and tell how shape affects function		
- identify structures on a neighbourhood or school walk		
- experiment with making simple pulleys		observation
- use tools to make a job easier		observation, interview
examine structures found in nature		
- explore fasteners at a Fix-It Centre		
- explore materials, tools, and fasteners at a Carpentry Centre		observation, interview
- design structures		observation, interview
- explore how various machines work		
- draw and describe playground structures	LM 1	interview, observation, portfolio
- build models of structures for a tabletop playground		observation
- create patterns by repeating a shape	LM 2	observation, portfolio
- sort structures by their function		observation
- build a structure with moving parts		observation
- draw and describe a fairground ride and the system that runs it	LM 3	portfolio
- with their families, design and build a skeletal structure	Family Letter Master B	
- find matching shapes within the Student Book		
- draw structures whose function is described	LM 4	rubric

PLANNING AHEAD

TEACHER RESOURCES

Harlen, Wynne. Developing Science in a Primary Classroom. London: Olive & Boyd, 1989.

Renner, John W., Marek, Edmund A. The Learning Cycle: Elementary School Science Teaching. Boston: Heinnemann Educational Books, 1988.

BOOKS FOR CHILDREN

Barton, Byron. Building a House. New York: Greenwillow, 1981.

Gibbons, Gail. Up Goes the Skyscraper! New York: Macmillian, 1986.

McGraw, Sheila. Pâpier Maché for Kids. Toronto: Firefly Books, 1991.

Morris, Ann. House and Homes. New York: Morrow, 1992.

Stevenson, Robert Louis. Block City. New York: Dutton, 1988.

WEB SITES

National Museum of Science and Technology: www.science-tech.nmstc.ca/english/schoolzone/tellmeabout.cfm

Look Learn & Do: www.looklearnanddo.com/documents/projects.html

CD-ROMS

Thinkin' Science by IBM. Win/Mac

Sammy's Science House by Edmark. Win/Mac

VIDEOS

My World ... Earth, McIntyre Media Ltd.

Cross-Curricular Overview

LINK TO...
SOCIAL STUDIES UNIT

ALL ABOUT RULES

After Activity 1, you might wish to do the second Student Book activity in **All About Rules** in Ginn Social Studies, where children create a class book of rules for the playground. Thinking about playground rules will help children as they build structures for a playground and consider how to use the structures to create a tabletop playground in Activity 2.

PLAYGROUND CIRCUIT

Curriculum Link: *Health and Physical Education*
Use anytime after: Activity 1

Purpose:
- Participate in moderate to vigorous physical activity for five to ten minutes.
- Identify the major parts of the body by their proper names.

Materials
- playground

Get Started

Explain to children that our bodies have more than 600 muscles. They tighten (contract) and loosen (relax) to allow our bodies to move and do activities. The more you exercise a particular muscle, the bigger and stronger it gets.

One at a time, ask a volunteer to jump up and down, another to pretend to throw a ball, and a third to do a situp. Ask children each time what muscles they think the volunteer is using (leg muscles, arm muscles, and stomach muscles).

Record children's responses, guiding them to the correct answers if they are not forthcoming.

Work On It

Tell the children that they are going to go out to the playground and find one activity that uses their leg muscles, one that uses their arm muscles, and one that uses their stomach muscles. Remind them that they are going to tell the class what they found out, so they should remember what they did for each muscle. Take the children to the playground to do the activity.

Communicate

Back in class, invite children to describe to the class what activities they did and what muscles they used. Ask:
- Did you sometimes use more than one muscle during an activity? Can you think of other activities that use your arm muscles? Leg muscles? Stomach muscles? All your muscles?

WHAT CAN YOU BUILD WITH SHAPES?

Curriculum Link:
Mathematics
Use any time after:
Activity 3

Purpose
- Use two-dimensional shapes to construct a picture.
- Explore and identify two-dimensional shapes using concrete materials and drawings.

Materials
- pattern blocks

Get Started

Arrange several pattern blocks into a simple design or picture. Ask:
- What shapes have I used to make my picture? What does my picture look like to you? How many blocks have I used?

Challenge children to think how they could make the same picture using more (fewer) blocks. Explore and discuss children's ideas.

Work On It

Provide children with pattern blocks. Invite them to use the blocks to create a simple design or picture. Ask:
- What did you make? What shapes did you use? How many blocks did you use?

Challenge children to cover their picture using some different pattern blocks.

Communicate

Invite children to show how they changed their pictures. Ask them:
- Did you use more blocks or fewer blocks the second time? What blocks could you use instead of the yellow hexagon? The red trapezoid? What are some different ways you made the hexagon?

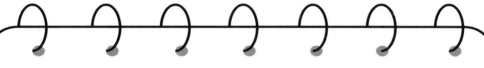

MAKE A MUSICAL PATTERN

Curriculum Link: *Music*
Use any time after: Activity 3

Purpose:
- Create rhythmic patterns using a variety of sounds.

Materials:
- simple instruments (optional)

Get Started

Clap or tap a simple pattern. Challenge the children to repeat it. After they have repeated it several times, ask a volunteer to clap another pattern, and invite the class to repeat it. Explain that these are sound patterns. A pattern is a series of objects or sounds that repeats. Ask:
• How else can we make sound patterns? What can we use to make sounds?

Record children's responses and keep the list posted for children to use as a reference.

Work On It

Divide the class into small groups, and invite each group to create a sound pattern. Children can use their bodies (clap, slap, tap, snap, stamp) or simple instruments such as sticks, triangles, or bells to create their sound patterns. Challenge them to come up with a name for each sound (snap, ding, ring, and so on), and to write their pattern.

Communicate

Invite each group to share its sound pattern with the class, and challenge the class to repeat it.

A LAUNCH THE TOPIC

Have children sit around a collection of blocks, empty tin cans, paper towel rolls, small cartons, and paper cups. Ask:

- Suppose you were interested in building a fence. How could you use these materials to build it?

Invite volunteers to come forward and demonstrate. Talk about why they chose the materials they did and why some of the materials are inappropriate. Ask:

- Suppose you wanted to build a bridge. What could you use?

Again volunteers can come forward and show the materials they would use and how they might attempt to place them. Discuss children's choices. Explain that the materials will be available for children to use during activity and science time. Encourage children to add to the collections so that there are many interesting materials to select for making structures.

KEEP IT GOING

Set aside a place for children to display the structures that they create on their own. Since children will eventually need to dismantle their creations, consider photographing them to create a permanent record of their endeavours. Encourage children to describe the shapes in their completed structures, the problems they encountered, and the solutions they found. While some children will have their own plans for building time, others may need a task to guide their efforts. Pose challenges like these as a prompt:

- What can you build to surround this car? How would you build a ramp for this car to travel down? What do you think is the longest wall you can build? The tallest tower? The strongest bridge?

As you begin this unit, send home Family Letter A. Encourage families to do some of the activities suggested to enhance children's learning about energy and its role in their lives.

B ACTIVITY BANK

1 SAME AND DIFFERENT

Purpose: - Compare form and function of structures.

Materials: 2 objects that are alike in some ways and different in others

Display two items that have the same form, such as an inflated balloon and a rubber ball. Ask:

- How are these the same? How are they different? Have children think of other things that are round.

Invite children to compare other items such as a tissue box and a brick, a chair and a table, a knapsack and a purse, and so on.

2 SHAPES ARE EVERYWHERE

PURPOSE: - Identify geometric shapes.

Play a game of I Spy in which clues describe the shapes of the object. For example, if you were describing a table you might say: I spy something that is a made of a large rectangle and has four legs.

Encourage children to make up clues. Explain that they must describe the shape of the structure in at least one of their clues.

3 WHAT HAPPENS?

PURPOSE: - Identify input and output of systems.

Play a game with children where you tell an action and they have to tell you the response. For example, point to the light switch and say: I am going to flick this switch. What will happen?

Continue with any other systems that you have in the class, or refer to familiar systems that children encounter in other settings, such as ringing a doorbell, opening the refrigerator door, and so on.

4 WHAT IS THIS FOR?

PURPOSE: - Recognize products are manufactured to meet a need.

MATERIALS: simple tool, such as a pencil

Display a tool, such as a pencil, and challenge the children to tell what it is made of, describe its shape, and explain how it is used. Record children's responses and challenge them to think of other things that match part of the description (for example, other things that are made of wood, other things that are long and thin, other things that you use to write).

5 WHAT IS IT?

PURPOSE: - Identify structures whose function is indicated by their shape.

MATERIALS: objects whose shape defines their functions

Invite children to identify objects by their shape. Choose an object, such as a key, keep it hidden from the children, and place it on the overhead projector. Cover it with a piece of paper so children still cannot see it. Turn on the projector, remove the paper, and ask:

- What do you think this mystery object is? How do you know?

Display another key and ask if the shapes are exactly alike. Have children consider why it would be a problem if every key were the same shape. Display objects, such as forks, spoons, pencils, and rulers, for children to identify.

6) STRUCTURE WALK

PURPOSE: - Classify various structures in their environment according to specific functions.

Take children on a walk around the school and neighbourhood where there are many different structures they can discuss. Invite children to identify structures and describe their size, shape, function, and the type of materials used to make them. Record their responses.

Children can illustrate some of their observations when they return to the classroom. Sort children's illustrations in a variety of ways, such as by size, material, function, or shape.

7) PULL THAT PULLEY

PURPOSE: - Describe how parts of some systems work together.

MATERIALS: simple pulleys
spools
large paper clips
string
scissors
coat hangers

Present different examples of pulleys and discuss with the children the different parts and how they work together. Provide each group with spools, large paper clips, string, scissors, and a coat hanger. Have small groups of children construct their own simple pulley. Ask each group to describe and demonstrate its pulley system.

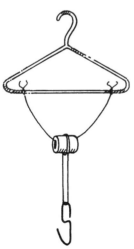

8) MAKE THE JOB EASIER

PURPOSE: - Select appropriate tools and utensils.

MATERIALS: small cups
cereal
variety of tools such as spoons,
tweezers, chopsticks, pipe cleaners,
craft sticks, clothespins

Provide each child with a small cup and a scoopful of cereal and challenge them to put the cereal into the cup without using their hands. Offer them a variety of tools, such as spoons, tweezers, chop sticks, pipe cleaners, craft sticks, and clothespins. Children can use the tools to do the job or to make another tool to do the job. When they are done, challenge them to do the task again with a different tool. Invite children to tell about the different tools and methods they used to do the job. Ask:

- Which tool was the easiest to use? The most difficult?

9) NATURE'S STRUCTURES

PURPOSE: - Distinguish between structures and devices made by man and structures found in nature.

MATERIALS: bird's nest or other natural structure
measuring tools
magnifying lenses

Animals are skillful builders. As children find examples of natural structures (nests, honeycombs) during this unit, invite them to examine and describe size, shape, materials, and patterns in those structures. Leave them on display along with tools such as measuring tapes and magnifying lenses for recording and observing.

10) WE CAN FIX IT!

PURPOSE: - Use tools appropriately when joining various materials.

MATERIALS: variety of fasteners

Set up a Fix-It Centre that includes tape, glue, stapler, masking tape, clothespins, screwdriver, and string. Have children look around the room and identify things that that they could fix themselves, such as ripped pages in a book, pictures or charts that are falling down, a torn story chart, or a ripped pillow. Encourage children to visit the Fix-It Centre for the tools and materials they need to get the job done.

SUSTAINABLE DEVELOPMENT

Is it better to fix an item or buy a new one? Why?

11 CARPENTERS AT WORK

PURPOSE:
- Select appropriate tools.
- Use tools appropriately when joining and shaping various materials.
- Use and recognize the effects of different finishing techniques and processes.
- Design and make different structures using concrete materials.

MATERIALS: carpentry materials

Set up a Carpentry Centre that includes wood scraps, safety goggles, small hammers, small nails (if desired), glue, measuring tapes, rulers, screws and screw driver, nuts and bolts, sandpaper, collage materials, and paint. Show the children the materials and explain and discuss necessary safety precautions.

Invite the children to work at the centre and to take their time to design, build, and finish projects. You may want to designate an area for storing works-in-progress.

Invite children to share their work. Questions such as these will prompt description of the process as well as the product:

- What did you make? What did you use? How did you attach the materials together? What did you do to finish it and make it look so nice? What problems did you have? How did you solve them? What else would you like to have at the Carpentry Centre?

12 ARCHITECTS AT WORK

Purpose:
- Design and make structures and use appropriate vocabulary to explain their function.

MATERIALS: different types of natural and manufactured building materials, as below

Create a Building Center where children have access to different types of natural and manufactured building materials, such as building blocks, commercial building toys, lids, small boxes, cords, craft sticks, spools, cardboard shapes, sticks and twigs, smooth wood pieces, and modelling clay.

Provide time for children to build freely so they can explore their own investigations. If you wish, pose a specific problem for children to explore, for example by asking:

- How would you build something that could hold something in it? How would you build a bridge? A tower? How would you build a structure that something could crawl under? Through?

Encourage children to display and describe their structures.

13 HOW DO THOSE MACHINES WORK?

PURPOSE:
- Describe how the parts of some systems work together.

MATERIALS: collection of simple machines, functional and broken

Create a display area where children can observe and describe the workings of simple machines, kitchen gadgets, and toys with wheels and gears. Provide broken machines, such as telephones and clocks, to give children a hands-on opportunity to observe the inner systems of more complex machines.

" Things we build are called structures. "

PURPOSE:

– Design and make different structures using concrete materials, and explain the function of the structure.

– Explain the function of a structure that they have made and describe how they made it.

– Explain the function of different structures.

– Record relevant observations.

– Identify structures whose function is indicated by their shape.

MATERIALS:

• collections of building materials from school and home (recycled materials such as cardboard boxes, cardboard tubes, plastic fruit containers)
• connecting blocks
• wooden blocks
• chart paper
• LM 1

TIME:

1 class period

SKILL FOCUS:

observing, communicating

GET STARTED

Provide pairs or small groups of children with a collection of building materials. Challenge them to work together to build a tall tower that won't fall down. Provide children with time to build and rebuild as they explore different ways to assemble the materials. Explain to children that what they are building is a structure. Anything that humans or animals build is called a structure. Ask:

■ Tell about your structure. What materials did you use? What did you do so that it wouldn't fall down?

WORK ON IT

USING PAGES 2-3

Invite children to look at the book. Ask:

■ What do you like to do at the playground? What would you like to do in this playground?

Encourage children to identify and describe the different structures in the picture. Ask:

■ What is each structure like? What is it used for? Are there any structures here like the one you built? How are they the same? Different?

BEYOND THE PAGE

Take children outdoors to examine the structures in the school playground or a local indoor or outdoor playground. Provide children with a copy of LM 1, a pencil, and a clipboard or other surface for drawing or writing. Ask:

■ What are these structures like? What are they used for? Do any of these structures remind you of ones you saw in our book? Ones you've built?

Ask children to choose a structure and make a detailed recording of what it looks like and what it can be used for. Encourage children to add as many descriptive words as they can.

COMMUNICATE

In class, ask children to tell about their work. Display their recordings with the chart.

ASSESSMENT OPPORTUNITY

Visit children as they build towers. Ask:
■ Why did you choose these materials? What other materials do you wish you had? What is the most important thing you need to remember when you try to build strong structures? Sturdy ones? Keep notes of children's responses on AM 3. Children's recordings of their **observations** are good **portfolio** entries. You can list entries on AM 4.

PURPOSE:

– Explain the function of different structures.

– Classify various structures in their environment by feature and function.

– Design and make structures.

– Ask questions about and identify needs or problems related to structures in their immediate environment.

– Plan investigations as responses.

– Use appropriate vocabulary to describe investigations.

– Communicate the procedures and results of investigations and explorations.

– Use appropriate natural and manufactured materials to make structures.

– Select appropriate tools and utensils.

MATERIALS:

• paper
• drawing materials
• materials for building skeletal and solid structures (straws, pipe cleaners, toothpicks, modelling clay, wood pieces, cardboard tubes, corks, tape, glue, string)
• materials for finishing and decorating

TIME:

1 class period

SKILL FOCUS:

interpreting, making models, communicating

" Build a structure for a model playground. "

GET STARTED

Create a chart with the headings: Slide, Climb, Swing, Balance, Hang. Read the words aloud and ask:

■ Where can you (slide) on a playground structure? (slide, pole, tilting tunnel)

Record children's responses under the corresponding word on the chart.
Post labels for the activities listed on the chart and read them aloud. Say:

■ We have talked about many activities that you do on playground structures. Are there any other activities you do there?

Add children's responses, then ask:

■ Which of these activities do most of you like to do best?

Invite children to draw themselves doing their favourite activity on squares of paper, large self-stick notes, or index cards. Post the drawings to create a picture graph. When the graph is complete ask:

■ What can you tell from this graph of playground activities?

WORK ON IT

USING PAGES 4 AND 5

Introduce children to the task of building a model of a playground structure.
Encourage them to talk about the structures they want to build. Before they begin, ask questions like these to help them focus their plans:

■ What will your structure be used for? How will people get on it? Does it attach to anything else? What materials do you need? What else do we need to collect? How will you make sure your structure is sturdy? How will you make sure it is stable enough to move to the table top?

Together, read the instructions on the page for making items for the tabletop playground. Make sure that children understand the directions.

BEYOND THE PAGE

Set up materials for building in a central location. Children may work alone, but may prefer to work in pairs or small groups. Provide children with time to build and revise their structures and to add any finishing touches they wish.

COMMUNICATE

Encourage children to tell or write about their structures. As a class discuss the challenges they had and how they overcame them. Have children tell how they would build a structure differently next time and what materials they would like to have.

EXTENSION

Encourage children to add other structures to the playground. They can also add props, such as small plastic people, trees, bikes, or items made from small commercial blocks.

ASSESSMENT OPPORTUNITY

Observe how well children can plan and create a structure. Are they able to build a sturdy structure? Are they able to describe the parts and function of their structure? Do they add finishing touches to their structure? Record your **observations** on AM 3.

" You can see shapes in structures. Sometimes shapes make a pattern. "

PURPOSE:

– Explain the function of different structures.

– Identify geometric shapes in ordinary structures.

– Describe patterns that are produced by the repetition of specific shapes or motifs in various materials and objects.

– Identify structures whose function is indicated by their shape.

MATERIALS:

• multiple sets of shapes cut from BLM 2
• paper
• drawing materials
• glue
• long strips of paper
• small boxes

TIME:

1 class period

SKILL FOCUS:

observing, classifying

GET STARTED

Engage children in describing objects and the shapes they see within them. Ask:

■ Where did you find squares? Which shape did we find in many structures? Which shape was not found a lot?

Post a set of shapes cut from LM 2. Ask:

■ What do we call these shapes? How are all triangles the same? All squares? All circles? All rectangles?

Give each child one of the shapes cut from LM 2. Challenge them to find as many of that shape in the classroom as they can and to draw each item they find on a separate sheet of paper.

Meet as a class and record children's observations by creating a separate chart for each shape. Post children's drawings and the name of the object on the correct chart.

WORK ON IT

USING PAGES 6 AND 7

Have children look at the illustration of the playground. Ask:

■ What shapes do you see? Did you find that shape in the classroom? What part of the structure is made using only one shape? Two shapes? Why do you think those shapes were used?

Next, explain to children that putting several shapes together can create a pattern. Point out the chain-link fence and describe its repeating pattern of diamonds. Ask:

■ What other patterns can you see here? Where do you see shapes being repeated to make a pattern? Where do you see different materials repeated to make a pattern?

BEYOND THE PAGE

Provide children with glue, paper, drawing materials, a collection of shapes cut from LM 2, long strips of paper, and small boxes. Explain to the children that they will be using shapes to create patterns to cover

a wall or a small playhouse to add to the model playground.

Have children choose the shapes they wish to use and stress to them that they need to combine their shapes to make a pattern. As children work, you can display examples that are underway.

COMMUNICATE

Encourage children to descibe the shapes used and the patterns that are emerging.

ASSESSMENT OPPORTUNITY

Pay attention to how children identify the shapes and patterns. Are they able to tell about their own work and to find the patterns in the work of others? Encourage them to describe the patterns by telling the shapes used. Record your **observations** on AM 1, AM 2, and AM 3, and store children's completed work in their **portfolios**.

PURPOSE:

– Identify ways in which various structures are similar to and different from others in form and function.

– Classify various structures in their environment according to specific features and functions.

– Use appropriate natural and manufactured materials to make structures.

– Select appropriate tools and utensils.

– Distinguish between structures and devices made by humans and structures found in nature.

MATERIALS:

• drawing materials
• paper
• collections of building materials and toys

TIME:

1 class period

SKILL FOCUS

comparing, classifying

"Structures that do the same thing can look different."

GET STARTED

Engage children in thinking about structures in the classroom by posing riddles like these:

■ It has four legs and a back. What is it? (chair) It has four legs and two sides. What is it? (easel)

Help children to understand more about structures by challenging them to make structures with their bodies, working in pairs. Give them directions like these to follow:

■ Use your bodies to build a bridge. How can you get together to build a table? Now change your table into a chair.

Encourage children to look around to see how other pairs respond. Invite children to tell how their responses are similar and different.

WORK ON IT

USING PAGES 8 AND 9

Read the pages together. Invite children to look at the pictures of structures, identify each one, and then ask them to compare each set. Focus their attention on appearance, material, shape, size, and function. Invite them to describe the set, beginning with the structure found in a playground. Ask:

■ Describe the playground bench. What is it used for? How is it the same as other things we sit on? How is it different?

Repeat for the other groups of structures on the pages, recording children's observations on chart paper.

BEYOND THE PAGE

Invite children to work in small groups. Have each group look around the room to find structures that are similar to one of the bench, table, and playhouse. Provide each group with a large piece of butcher paper and encourage them to draw a poster showing the things they find.

Children may wish to add to their posters by including structures they have seen elsewhere in the school, on the playground, at home, in the community, and so on.

COMMUNICATE

Invite groups to share their poster with the class. Encourage children to describe how the structures they drew are similar to the ones in the Student Book and how they differ. Display children's posters on a bulletin board.

EXTENSION

Take a walk through the school and around the schoolyard. Challenge children to find structures made by people and structures that are part of nature, such as a tree or a bird's nest. Encourage children to compare the two kinds of structures.

ASSESSMENT OPPORTUNITY

By now children have had several opportunities to compare structures and explore their functions. Consider who can find similarities and differences among the common structures, who can identify structures, and who can communicate their observations clearly. Record your **observations** on AM 1.

" Some structures have parts that move. "

PURPOSE:

- Describe, using their own experience, how the parts of some systems work together.
- Design and make different structures and explain their function.
- Ask questions about and identify needs or problems related to structures in their immediate environment.
- Plan investigations to respond.
- Use appropriate vocabulary to describe investigations.
- Communicate the procedures and results of investigations and explorations.
- Use appropriate natural and manufactured materials to make structures.
- Select appropriate tools and utensils.

MATERIALS:

- objects with moving parts (can opener, toy car, hand mixer, objects that use pulleys or springs or that show gears)
- building materials

TIME:

2 class periods

SKILL FOCUS:

observing, making models, experimenting, communicating

GET STARTED

Place the collection of objects with moving parts at a centre in the classroom. Invite children to visit the centre and to explore the items there. Some children may even wish to bring in items to add to the collection. Encourage children to examine how the different parts work together.

Invite children to share with the group any observations they have made during their exploration. Questions like these can further guide their discoveries:

- What part did you move? What happens to the other parts when you do that? Why? What happens to the whole object when you do that?

WORK ON IT

USING PAGES 10 AND 11

Before turning to pages 10 and 11, ask children to look back at previous pages to find any objects that may have moving parts. List their responses. Discuss the parts that move and how they influence other parts and the whole.

Look at the pictures on pages 10 and 11. Ask:

- What do you have to do to start moving the (swing)? What other moving parts do you see on the page?

Together, read the instructions on the page to make sure everyone understands the task. Encourage children to look closely at the items on the page and decide what they want to build. Ask:

- What materials do you need to build a (swing)?

BEYOND THE PAGE

Provide a variety of materials at a centre and ensure that children know they can find what they need there. Children can work alone, in pairs, or in a group.

Give children time to build their structures, and to test them, revise them, and add any necessary finishing touches.

COMMUNICATE

Invite children to share their structure with the class. Encourage them to describe what they built, how the moving part works, and what materials they used. As a class discuss the challenges they had and how they overcame them. Have children tell how they would build a structure differently next time and what materials they would like to have.

EXTENSION

Bring in examples of pulleys for children to examine. Set one up in the room as a message system which takes notes from one side of the room to the other.

Interested children can make a pulley system using a spool, string, a wire hanger, and a large paper clip.

ASSESSMENT OPPORTUNITY

Observe children as they build to find out more about how well they handle unexpected challenges. Who is able to integrate the ideas of others into plans and model-building? Who perseveres and does not give up when challenges are presented? Who sees the work to completion and takes pride in the final product? Record your **observations** on AM 3.

PURPOSE:

– Identify the action required to operate an everyday system, and identify the response of that system.

– Describe, using their own experience, how the parts of some systems work together.

MATERIALS:

• drawing materials
• paper
• BLM 3

TIME:

1 class period

SKILL FOCUS:

observing

" Many structures at the fair move. You can turn them on and off. "

GET STARTED

Engage children in thinking about how parts of systems work together by asking three to six children to stand. Have them line up so that they can touch the person in front of them easily. Start the "system" by tapping the first child in line. That child performs a motion and then lightly taps the next child. The next child begins a motion. The first child does not stop, but keeps repeating his or her motion. This keeps going until everyone in line is moving in some way. Stop the "system" by tapping the last child and having each child tapped in turn to stop his or her motion.

To demonstrate systems at work in the classroom, begin to turn things on and off, such as overhead lights, a computer, a tape recorder. Ask:

• What did I just do? What happened after I switched this off? On? What other things do you do to make things work?

Record the ideas on a chart. Keep it posted and add to it as children think of additional ideas.

WORK ON IT

USING PAGES 12 AND 13

Invite children to look at the pages and identify the things that turn on and off, and how they work. Remind them of the

"tapping" system they created, and encourage them to look for things on the fairground that are part of a system. Ask:

• How do the (cars) work? How do they start? Stop?

Record children's responses on chart paper. Invite them to identify other things that turn on and off, and add them to the list. Children may wish to bring to school photographs or magazine cutouts of amusement park rides to add to the chart.

SUSTAINABLE DEVELOPMENT

Where does each structure get its energy? Which structure do you think is best for the environment?

BEYOND THE PAGE

Provide each child with a copy of LM 3. Explain that the on/off switch on it operates another ride on a fairground. Challenge children to draw any ride they wish—one they have seen or one they make up—that would be operated by the switch.

COMMUNICATE

Invite children to share their work with the class. Encourage them to describe what they drew, what kind of motion it has, and how it starts and stops.

Post children's work on a bulletin board or create a class book.

ASSESSMENT OPPORTUNITY

Children's drawings are good **portfolio** entries. They provide insight into how well children can communicate their ideas on paper and are evidence of children's thinking about how parts move together.

PURPOSE:

– Design and make different structures using concrete materials, and explain the function of the structure.

– Identify geometric shapes in ordinary structures.

– Use tools appropriately when joining and shaping various materials.

MATERIALS:

• modelling clay
• Family Letter B (optional)

TIME:

1 to 2 class periods

SKILL FOCUS:

making models, comparing

At Home

GET STARTED

Encourage children to think about the different structures they have observed during the course of this unit, and to review the structures they have built. If there are structures displayed in the classroom, children can spend a few minutes looking at them.

WORK ON IT

USING PAGES 14 AND 15

Together, examine pages 14 and 15. Ask:
- What materials are we going to use for this structure? Has anyone ever built something with toothpicks and clay before? Tell us about it.

Together, brainstorm a list of possible structures (bridge, tower, ladder, jungle gym) to get children thinking of what they might like to build.

Send home either the Student Book or Family Letter B so families can work together to build structures. You might

consider providing children and their families with modelling clay and toothpicks in small resealable bags. If you choose to do this activity in class, set aside a place for children to display their completed structures. Suggest that children build their structures on a piece of cardboard so they are easy to move.

COMMUNICATE

Have children present their completed structures. Children who are transporting structures back to school should do so using a container such as a shoe box. Ask questions like these to foster discussion:
- What problems did you have? How did you fix them? Why did you choose this structure to build? What did you learn about structures and building that you didn't know before? Tell about the different shapes and patterns in your structure. How are the structures we made alike? How are they different? What does your structure remind you of?

PURPOSE:

– Identify geometric shapes in ordinary structures.

SKILL FOCUS:

observing

Look Back

WORK ON IT

USING PAGE 16

Together, read page 16 in the Student Book and ensure that everyone understands the task. Have children complete the activity on the page.

ANSWERS

The children will find
- the hexagon in the climber on page 3
- the ride platform (circle) on page 13
- the tire (circle) on the spring-mounted red car in the playground on page 2
- the square of modelling clay on page 15
- the triangle in the climber on page 3
- the diamond in the chain link fence on pages 2 and 3
- the roof shingle (rectangle) on page 3

Some of the shapes from pages 2-3 also appear on pages 6-7 and 8-9.

COMMUNICATE

Invite children to share what they found, and to talk about what they learned about structures.

ASSESSMENT OPPORTUNITY

Provide children with a copy of AM 5 for self-assessment. Discuss children's answers with them individually, and store completed Assessment Masters in children's portfolios.

Demonstrate What You Know

PURPOSE:

– Assess children's learning.

MATERIALS:

• building blocks or other simple building materials
• LM 4 for each child
• drawing or writing materials, scissors

SKILL FOCUS:

observing, classifying

GET STARTED

Using building blocks or materials such as small cartons, paper towel rolls, and tin cans, build a structure in front of the children. Focus their attention on the structure by asking:

■ What does this structure remind you of? What shapes can you find in it? Can you find a square shape? A shape of a triangle?

After children have observed and described the structure, have them close their eyes as you change it by removing something from, or adding something to, it. Have them open their eyes and ask:

■ How has the structure changed?

Once the change is identified you can repeat with children taking turns in the role of builder.

ASSIGN THE TASK

Distribute LM 4 to the children and explain what they are to find for each section. Explain that they can use words or pictures to show what they find. You might find it best to do each section as a whole class to make sure that the instructions are clear. Think about whether you want to do this in the classroom, outdoors, or in another setting such as the library.

Take a look at the children's completed sheets and record your observations of their work. Then, invite children to cut their sheets so that the four sections are separate. On separate sheets of chart paper print the same sentences that appear on LM 4. Invite children to post their responses on the large sheets. Ask:

■ Did anyone think of the same climbing structure that you did? The same structure with square shapes?

Have children suggest other types of structures that might fit in each category. If children find those structures, they can add the names to the appropriate chart.

ASSESS THE TASK

The following rubric will help you to assess each child's learning about structures.

Performance Task Rubric	
Rubric	**Criteria**
Level 4	• child observes and records a structure for climbing, a structure with square shapes, a structure for sitting on, and a structure an animal makes • child communicates observations and comparisons clearly
Level 3	• child observes and records three or four of the structures that meet the given criteria • child communicates some observations and comparisons
Level 2	• child observes and records one or two of the structures that meet the given criteria • child requires assistance throughout to communicate observations and comparisons
Level 1	• child observes and records no structures that meet the given criteria • child is unable to identify any similarities or differences in structures

Family Letter (A)

Dear Family,

We will be learning about many types of structures. We will discuss how structures can be the same and how they are different. We will look for shapes and patterns in a variety of human-made and natural structures. Ask your child to tell you about the different structures he or she is making in class.

Here are some other activities that you can do at home to extend and reinforce our science curriculum. I hope that you enjoy them!

▶ Play "I Spy" with your child, using shapes in the clues. For example: I spy an object that is a large square. It is divided into four smaller squares. It is clear and you can see through it. What do I spy? (window) Encourage your child to take on the role of spy.

▶ If you have scraps of wood, encourage your child to sand them and use them to construct something. Discuss different ways that the pieces can be joined together, offering help as needed.

▶ Look for different structures at the park. What shapes can you find in them? Your child should be able to describe different structures by telling about the shapes and patterns in them. Look for natural structures such as a bird's nest or spider web. Don't disturb—just observe.

▶ Encourage your child to build structures with blocks. Pose a challenge such as: What is the tallest tower you can build? How can you build a bridge between these two chairs? What type of box can you make for your toys? Encourage your child to describe the completed structure and to point out the different shapes created.

✂ ---

AT THE PLAYGROUND

Family Letter (B)

Dear Family,

We have begun discussing the following activity in the classroom, and hope you will enjoy completing the activity with your child.

Use toothpicks and modelling clay to build a structure. Brainstorm with your child what structure you would like to build.

Copyright © 2000 Pearson Education Canada Inc.

Name: _____   Date: _____

I Saw a Structure

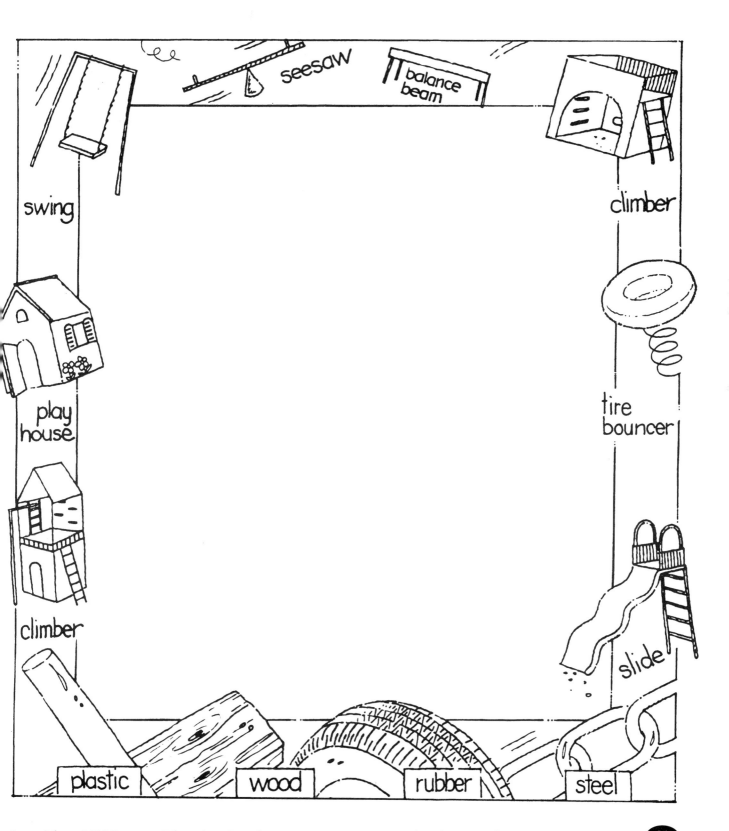

Copyright © 2000 Pearson Education Canada Inc.   At the Playground   **85**

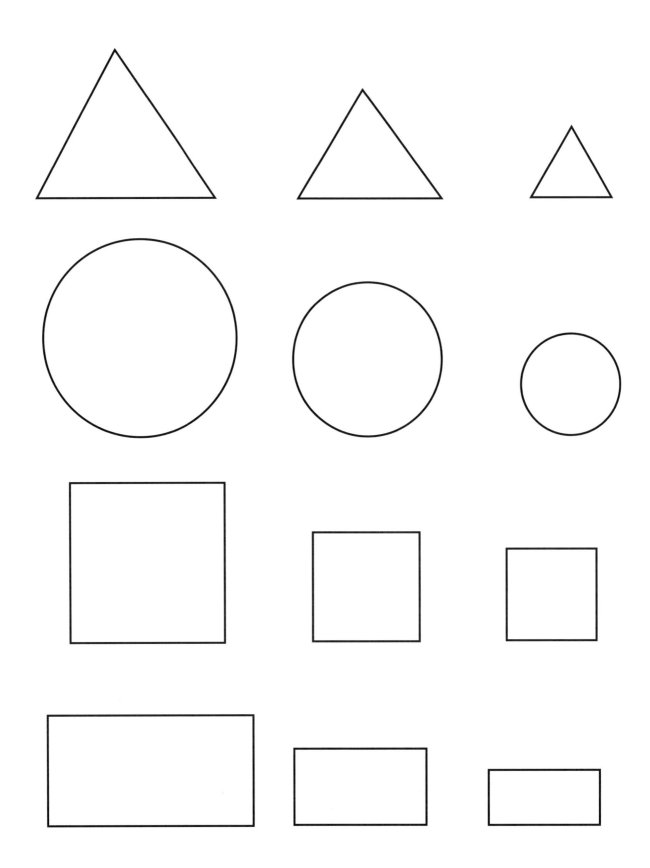

 Copyright © 2000 Pearson Education Canada Inc.

Name: _____   Date: _____

What does this switch turn on?

Name:
Draw a structure that you climb.

Name:
Draw a structure that you sit on.

Name:
Draw a structure that has square shapes in it.

Name:
Draw a structure that an animal makes.

 Copyright © 2000 Pearson Education Canada Inc.

Energy for Work and Play

UNIT OVERVIEW

This unit introduces children to some forms of energy and ways in which they are used in daily life.

- **Children learn** that the sun is the principal source of energy for all living things. They begin to appreciate that the food we eat grows because of heat and light from the sun.

- **Children continue to explore** forms of energy through the familiar context of toys—those that use human energy through a push or pull, as well as those that use energy from the wind, batteries, or electricity.

- **Children investigate** how energy can be stored and released to make a toy work before designing and building a simple toy of their own.

- Finally, **children recognize** other ways we use energy in our daily lives, and develop an understanding of our dependence on energy by planning a day without electricity. They also think of ways to reduce our use of electricity.

CONCEPT DEVELOPMENT AND OTHER ISSUES

Sources of energy and energy consumption are abstract concepts for children of this age. You might find age-appropriate materials about energy through your local power provider. The following suggestions may also help clarify the concept:

Do the activity School Energy Tour on page 95.

Consider a trip to a local farm or garden nursery where farmers or gardeners can help explain the link between the sun and the food we eat.

Plan a trip to a solar-heated building in your area so children can see how the sun can heat buildings and help us reduce consumption of non-renewable resources such as oil.

If any families in the school community are working to reduce their household energy consumption, invite them to class to share their strategies with the children.

COLLECTING MATERIALS

You will need a varied collection of *wind-up toys*, and *push and pull toys*, for children to explore. Your collection might also include *solar-powered items, such as watches and calculators*, for children to observe, use, and investigate. Here are some ideas for ensuring a rich collection.

- Encourage children to bring *simple push, pull*, and *wind-up toys* from home. Make sure that all toys are labelled with the child's name.

- Collect *small wind-up toys* from family, friends, and staff members.

- Fast-food restaurants often feature small, inexpensive *wind-up toys*. Contact local businesses to obtain some of these toys for school use.

A collection of toys will attract children's attention, so set aside time for them to demonstrate and explain the toys they bring to class. You might find it best to display toys only during science time.

You will also need a bulletin board space for the first activity. Have magazines and brochures available throughout the unit so children can search for pictures to add to this display.

Unit Planner

ACTIVITY FOCUS → CHILDREN:	TIME	MATERIALS
(A) LAUNCH THE TOPIC ACTIVITY		
do physical activities to access knowledge about energy; create a word web and questions for inquiry and investigation	1 class period	chart paper
(B) ACTIVITY BANK ACTIVITIES		
❶ Energy Control — describe how senses help us control energy-using devices	Take 5	
❷ Food as an Energy Source — identify food as a source of energy for living things		
❸ In and Out — operate a simple device or system and identify input and output		simple electric devices (computer, hair dryer, radio, overhead projector)
❹ The Sun's Energy — recognize that the sun is the principal source of energy on Earth		solar calculator, pictures of solar panels
❺ School Energy Tour — describe forms of energy used in everyday devices; identify devices controlled manually	Take 30	
❻ Energy Detectives — identify everyday uses of energy; list things they can do to reduce energy consumption		
❼ Lights Out — select a common form of energy and predict the effect if it were not there		writing and colouring materials
❽ Sunlight and Growing Things — recognize that the sun is the principal source of energy on Earth	Take Time	2 similar plants
❾ Moving Things — construct a manually controlled device that performs a certain task		construction paper, table tennis balls, small objects
(C) STUDENT BOOK/FLIP CHART BOOK ACTIVITIES		
❶ All living things get energy from the sun. — *pages 2-3* recognize the sun as our main source of energy	1 class period	solar-powered calculator or watch, magazines, flyers, catalogues, scissors
❷ Energy makes toys work. — *pages 4-5* identify the energy source for a variety of toys	1 class period	several toys that work manually, chart paper, scissors, glue, paper
❸ How do wind-up toys work? — *pages 6-7* investigate stored energy	1 class period	one small wind-up toy, measuring tool
❹ Make a toy. — *pages 8-9* construct a manually controlled device that performs a specific task.	2 to 3 class periods	paper, drawing materials, chart paper, variety of craft materials
❺ Some toys use electricity and batteries. — *pages 10-11* identify common energy sources	2 class periods	chart paper, magazines, catalogues, scissors, glue, paper
❻ Electricity makes lots of things work. — *pages 12-13* explore alternatives to electricity use	2 class periods	list of things that switch on and off from previous activity, drawing materials
❼ At Home — *pages 14-15* identify everyday uses of energy, list things they can do to reduce energy consumption	equivalent to 1 class period	
❽ Look Back — *page 16* reflect on and synthesize what they know	1 class period	
(D) DEMONSTRATE WHAT YOU KNOW TASK		
❶ identify everyday uses of energy, predict the effect if common forms of energy were not there	1 class period plus	energy web from Keep It Going, drawing and writing materials

ACTIVITY DESCRIPTION — CHILDREN:	LINE MASTERS	ASSESSMENT
- expend energy and discuss the meaning of energy; create a 'Know/Wonder/Learned' chart	Family Letter Master A	
- tell how our senses help us control energy		
- discuss how living things use food for energy		
- tell how we make simple devices work		
- learn how solar cells work		
- tour the school to see energy sources		
- note where energy can be saved in the school or neighbourhood		
- list objects that can and can't be used without electricity		observation
- compare plant growth when sunlight is removed		
- make a fan and use it to move objects		observation, interview
- make a bulletin board showing food sources		observation
- sort toys by their energy source	LM 1	portfolio, observation
- experiment with a wind-up toy	LM 2	observation
- plan and make a toy using a variety of materials		observation, portfolio
- sort pictures of items by their energy source		observation
- plan a day without electricity	LM 3	portfolio
- identify electrical devices at home and make posters about energy conservation	Family Letter Master B	
- identify the energy sources in an unusual machine		
- identify items that could not be used without electricity, complete an energy web	LM 4	rubric

PLANNING AHEAD

TEACHER RESOURCES

Richards, Roy. An Early Start to Technology. New York: Simon & Schuster, 1992.

Sprung, Barbara, Froschl, Merle, and Campbell, Patricia B. What Will Happen If ... ? Young Children and the Scientific Method. New York: Educational Equity, 1985.

BOOKS FOR CHILDREN

Baisch, Chris. When the Lights Went Out. New York: G.P. Putnam's Sons, 1987.

Branley, Franklyn M. The Sun: Our Nearest Star. New York: Harper & Row, 1988.

Calhoun, Mary. Jack and the Whoopee Wind. New York: William Morrow, 1987.

Charles, Veronika Martenova. Hey! What's That Sound? Toronto: Stoddart Publishing, 1994.

WEB SITES

Energy Quest: www.energy.ca.gov/education

Let's Talk Science: www.letstalkscience.uwo.ca/programs/educators/index.html

CD-ROMS

I Love Science by DK Multimedia. Win/Mac

VIDEOS

The Green House, B.C. Learning Connection Inc.

Light, B.C. Learning Connection Inc.

Cross-Curricular Overview

LINK TO...
SOCIAL STUDIES UNIT

PEOPLE AT WORK

After Activity 1 in the Student Book, you may wish to do Activity 5 in **People at Work** in Ginn Social Studies, where children have the opportunity to find out more about how workers get our food to us.

FOUR FOOD GROUPS

Curriculum Link: *Health and Physical Education*
Use any time after: Activity 1

Purpose:
- Identify the four food groups and give examples of foods in each group.

Materials:
- variety of foods from the four food groups (or pictures or models of foods)
- copy of Canada's Food Guide to Healthy Eating
- hoops, yarn, sorting mat, or other tool for sorting into 4 groups

Get Started

One at a time, show the children the food items you have brought to class. Invite them to identify each one.

Show children a copy of Canada's Food Guide to Healthy Eating. Explain to them that this guide divides foods into four groups (Grain Products, Vegetables and Fruit, Milk Products, and Meat and Alternatives), and that healthy eating means eating foods from each group every day.

Work On It

Set out the sorting tool. Hold up one food item at a time and ask:

- Which food group does this belong to?

Sort the foods according to children's responses.

Communicate

As children match foods to food groups, encourage them to explain their choice. Once all foods are sorted, ask:

- Are all of these foods sorted in the right place? How do you know? Would you sort any of these foods in other groups? Why?

Revise children's work as necessary. Then ask:

- What other foods belong in each group?

Invite children to draw the other foods they have mentioned and to sort them.

HOW BIG IS IT?

Curriculum Link: *Mathematics*
Use any time after: Activity 3

Purpose
- Estimate, measure and record the linear dimensions of objects using non standard units.

Materials
- a variety of toys or stuffed animals
- measuring tools such as string, linking cubes, craft sticks, straws

Get Started
Display a variety of toys. Ask:

- Why might someone need to know how big a toy is?

After discussing their ideas tell children they will have a chance to measure one of these toys. Focus their attention on the measuring tools and choose one for demonstration. Ask:

- How can you use (these craft sticks) to measure the length of this (push toy)?

As children measure the toy, reinforce the starting point and aligning the non standard units so they touch end to end. Ask:

- How long is the toy?

Work On It
Give children a toy or stuffed animal to measure. Ask them to select a measuring tool, estimate the length or height and then measure. Discuss ways to record what they did and what they found out.

Communicate
As children share their work, ask:

- What did you use to measure? What was your estimate? What did you find out? Was the toy longer or shorter than you thought?

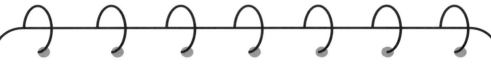

I CAN BE ...

Curriculum Link: *Drama and Dance*
Use any time after: Activity 5

Purpose:
- Demonstrate control of their bodies when moving like different objects.

Get Started
Refer children to any lists created throughout the unit of items that are powered by various forms of energy, such as gasoline, electricity, batteries, and so on. Invite children to add to the lists if they wish.

Work On It
Have a volunteer choose one item on the list. Then invite the whole class to pretend to be that item, making the sound and movement that item would make. Continue the activity, choosing a different item each time.

Communicate
After children have had the opportunity to be different objects, ask:

- What did you do to show that you were a (lawn mower)? How did you move? What kind of sound did you make?

Encourage children who are interested to pretend to be any object they choose and one at a time, challenge the class to guess what they are.

A LAUNCH THE TOPIC

Energy and its role in our daily lives is something that young children have not spent much time exploring on their own. However, they have probably heard the word in reference to their own behaviour. You can begin this science unit by finding out some of the impressions that children have formed about the concept of energy.

Have children stand in an open area. Ask them to start jogging slowly on the spot. Ask them to speed up, then to slow down. Have them come to a stop and ask:

- What did we just do? What happens when you jog for a short time? For a long time?

Ask the children to hop on the spot for a few minutes. Have them do some jumping jacks. Ask:

- What do you use when you do these kinds of things?

If the answer (energy) is not forthcoming, say, "You use energy when you exercise, play, or do sports."

Encourage children to tell about times when they have heard people talk about their energy, for example: "I have no energy." "You have so much energy today." "Where do you get all your energy?" Discuss what they think these things mean. Ask:

- When else have you heard people talk about energy? What do you think energy is?

KEEP IT GOING

Print the word energy as the centre of a web. Create the web using the words that children offer in their discussion about energy. Keep the web posted throughout the unit for children to add to or to edit.

Encourage children to pose any I Wonder questions about the topic of energy. Ask:

- What things would you like to find out about energy?

Record children's questions and revisit them as you work through the unit.

As you begin this unit, send home Family Letter A. Encourage families to do some of the activities suggested to enhance children's learning about energy and its role in their lives

B ACTIVITY BANK

1 ENERGY CONTROL

PURPOSE: –Describe how our senses of touch, hearing, and sight help us control energy-using devices in the home, school, and community.

Explain to the children that our senses help us control energy, for example when we hear the clock alarm, we turn it off. Point out how we use our senses to help us control energy in the classroom. On a sunny day ask:

■ Do we need the lights on to see our work? Why? (sun makes classroom bright) What should we do? (turn out lights)

2 FOOD AS AN ENERGY SOURCE

PURPOSE: –Identify food as a source of energy for themselves and other living things.

Explain to the children that food is our source of energy. Help children make this connection during the daily classroom routine. At snack time or recess, explain that children's snacks help give them energy. When children return from the gym ask:

■ How could you get back some of the energy you just used?

Link this discussion to ways that other living things get energy. Ask:

■ How does a cow get energy? What food does it eat? How does a flower get energy?

Repeat these kinds of questions whenever appropriate.

3 IN AND OUT

PURPOSE: –Operate a simple device or system and identify the input and the output.
–Identify devices that are controlled manually.

MATERIALS: some simple electric devices (cassette recorder, computer, hair dryer, radio or overhead projector)

Show the children the devices you have collected. Ask:

■ What is the same about all of these things? What do they all need to work? (electricity)

Plug in one device and have a volunteer turn it on. Ask:

■ What is needed to make it work? (electricity, someone to turn it on) Now that the electricity has gone into the machine, what comes out? (heat from a hair dryer; sound from a radio; light from an overhead projector)

Write Heat, Light, and Sound on chart paper and ask the children to sort the machines into these energy categories. Encourage them to think of other things that belong in each. Keep the lists posted so that children can add to them.

Energy		
Heat	Sound	Light
hair dryer	radio	overhead projector
toaster	tape deck	computer screen
oven	CD player	ceiling lights

4 THE SUN'S ENERGY

PURPOSE: –Recognize that the sun is our principal source of energy used on the surface of Earth.

MATERIALS: pictures of solar panels on buildings solar-powered calculators

Show children pictures of solar panels on rooftops. Explain that the energy from the sun is sometimes used to heat buildings. The panels collect heat from the sun to warm water below the roof. This warmed water moves through the building to heat it.

Provide the children with solar-powered calculators to explore. Explain that they do not get energy from batteries but rather from the sun's light. Have children cup their hands over the solar cells to see the result of light energy being removed. Encourage the children to think about whether the calculators would work outdoors on a dark night with no light source.

Energy for Work and Play —————— **95**

5) SCHOOL ENERGY TOUR

PURPOSE:
– Describe the different forms of energy used in a variety of everyday devices.
– Identify everyday devices that are controlled manually.

Arrange for children to go on a tour of the school building to look for uses of energy. Your school custodian is probably the best tour guide. Inform the custodian that you are studying energy use and want the children to get a better appreciation of the different sources of energy in use at the school. Before the tour, have children brainstorm questions such as:

■ Where are the electrical panels? Where is the furnace? How do you turn the furnace on and off? Does the furnace use gas or oil? Is any part of the school heated with electricity? Is there any way that the school is cooled in warm weather? Is there anything we can do to use less energy in the school?

6) ENERGY DETECTIVES

PURPOSE:
– Identify everyday uses of energy.
– Identify devices they use that consume energy and list things they can do to reduce energy consumption.

Take the children on a walk through the school or the immediate neighbourhood. Ask them to point out things that use energy, including people, and challenge the children to identify their source of energy. As an extra challenge, encourage children to point out where energy could be saved, such as turning off an idling car, daytime house lights, an unused computer, and so on.

7) LIGHTS OUT

PURPOSE:
– Select one of the most common forms of energy used every day and predict the effect on their lives if it were no longer available.

MATERIALS: writing and colouring materials

Explain to the children that they will be going on an imaginary camping trip tomorrow. There will be no electricity, but there are other forms of energy that they

can use. Encourage the children to make a list at home that evening of all the things that they won't be able to use on the camping trip. In class, list their ideas on the board. Beside each item listed encourage children to offer alternatives; for example, listing campfire beside stove, flashlight beside light, and so on. Invite children to draw a picture of a campsite that has some of these non-electrical alternatives. Post these drawings.

Our Camping Trip	
Can't Use	**Can Use**
stove	fire
lights	flashlight
clock	sun

8) SUNLIGHT AND GROWING THINGS

PURPOSE:
– Recognize that the sun is the principal source of energy used on the surface of Earth.

MATERIALS: two similar plants

To further establish the role of the sun as our principal source of energy, engage children in an investigation of how plants need sunlight to thrive. Ask:

■ What do you think a plant needs to grow and stay healthy?

List children's responses. Explain that they will be exploring how plants use energy from the sun. Place one of two similar plants on a window ledge. Place the other plant in a spot away from natural sunlight, preferably in a dark place such as a filing cabinet drawer or a closet. Explain that to find out if sunlight helps plants grow you must treat the plants exactly the same, except for the amount of sunlight. With the children's help, establish a watering schedule and an amount of water that is the same for both plants. At the beginning and end of each week, observe the plants. Discuss how they are changing and whether one plant seems to be healthier than the other.

9 MOVING THINGS

PURPOSE:
- Construct a manually controlled device that performs a specific task.
- Communicate the procedures and results of investigations and explorations for specific purposes, using demonstrations, drawings, and oral and written descriptions.

MATERIALS: construction paper
table tennis balls
small objects

Provide each child with a piece of paper and demonstrate how to fold it to make a fan. Discuss the fan and ask:

- What does it do? (cools you down) How does it work?

Give the children time to use their fans. Through discussion, establish that fans like these move air and that the moving air or wind can help cool you down. Extend the exploration of energy by challenging children to use the moving air, created by the fan, to move an object. Place a table tennis ball on the tabletop and ask:

- Do you think your fan could move this ball?

Call on volunteers to use their fans to move the ball. Ask:

- What is moving the ball? (wind made when the fan moves the air around it)

Make something that moves things

Challenge the children to find other things that they can move using their fan and encourage them to keep a record of these things.

Children can continue this investigation by designing and constructing other devices that make things move. Place materials for their use, such as straws, toothpicks, craft sticks, paper, tape, and scissors, in a central spot. Invite children to show what they have constructed and describe how it works.

You can also invite the children to look around the playground to see examples of things that move people, such as a seesaw, swings, and so on.

> ## All living things get energy from the sun.

PURPOSE:

– Recognize that the sun is the principal source of energy used on the surface of Earth.

– Identify food as a source of energy for themselves and other living things.

MATERIALS:

• solar-powered calculator or watch
• magazines
• flyers
• catalogues
• scissors

TIME:

1 class period

SKILL FOCUS:

observing, classifying

GET STARTED

Show children a solar-powered calculator or watch. Ask:

▪ Does anyone know how this works?

Explain that the energy from the sun, or from another light source, makes this work. Then ask:

▪ Who has a lot of energy today? Did you eat breakfast? What did you eat? Who doesn't feel like he or she has a lot of energy? Did you eat breakfast? What did you eat?

Explain that we get our energy indirectly from the sun. The heat and light from the sun make plants grow. We eat plants. Some animals eat plants. We eat animals, too. The food we eat gives us energy to do everything from sitting to playing to growing.

WORK ON IT

USING PAGES 2 AND 3

Invite children to look at the pages. Have them look closely at the illustrations. Invite volunteers to explain what they see and to describe how the sun is giving energy in each picture. (The sun makes the grass, vegetables, and seeds grow. The animals eat the grass and seeds. We eat the vegetables. We get milk from the cow. We eat the chicken. These foods give us energy and help us grow.)

BEYOND THE PAGE

Ask:

▪ What kinds of plants do you eat? What foods do you eat that come from animals?

Children's responses may include different fruits and vegetables, eggs, milk, cheese, and meat. Explain to them that the breads and grain products we eat also come from plants. Record answers throughout the

discussion to keep track of their thinking.

Provide the children with magazines, catalogues, flyers, and so on from which they can cut pictures. Invite them to look for pictures of foods they eat that come from plants, and foods they eat that come from animals (milk, eggs, cheese, meats). Have the children cut out pictures.

COMMUNICATE

Invite children to share their cutouts with the class. Encourage them to describe how the item they cut out gets its energy from the sun, and how it, in turn, gives energy to people.

Create a bulletin board with a large cutout of the sun in the centre. Paste children's cutouts around it.

EXTENSION

Hospitals, schools, farms, and even some homes in your area may make use of solar panels. Arrange a visit to a building that uses solar heating. Invite the owner or custodian to show the class how the system works.

SUSTAINABLE DEVELOPMENT

Why is it better to get energy from solar panels than from electricity?

ASSESSMENT OPPORTUNITY

To find out about children's ability to recognize the sun as the principal source of energy, you can **listen** to comments they make and the questions they pose during class discussions. **Observe** to see if they cut out appropriate pictures, and ask them to list or draw pictures to show what they need to get energy. You can record your findings on AM 1.

PURPOSE:

- Identify everyday uses of energy.
- Operate a simple device and identify the input and output.
- Identify everyday devices that are controlled manually.

MATERIALS:

- several toys that work manually (balls, gliders, pull-toys)
- chart paper
- LM 1 for each child
- scissors
- glue
- paper

TIME:

1 class period

SKILL FOCUS:

classifying

"Energy makes toys work."

GET STARTED

Collect several toys that work manually, such as balls, gliders, pull toys, and so on. Display the toys and invite volunteers to demonstrate how each toy works. Ask:

- What would the instructions for working this toy be?

Record children's suggestions on chart paper. When each toy has a set of instructions, read a set aloud. Ask:

- Which toy belongs to this set of instructions? Continue until each toy is matched with a set of instructions.

WORK ON IT

USING PAGES 4 AND 5

Invite children to describe the toys they see on the page. Ask:

- What is the same about all of these toys? What is different about them? Which one would you like to play with? Why?

Accept all responses, but ensure that children recognize that the energy that makes all of these toys work comes from people.

Make a chart with the headings Push and Pull. Challenge children to tell you under which column each toy belongs. Record their answers. Note that toys that need the wind often need a push as well. Have the children complete the chart by adding the

names of the toys from your collection. Ask:

- What other toys can you think of to add to this chart? Where do they belong?

Record children's answers.

BEYOND THE PAGE

Distribute LM 1 to each child and have the children cut the pictures apart. Invite children to sort the toys by how they work, then to share their decisions with one another and with you. When they are confident with their groupings, they can glue the pictures in place on a piece of construction paper.

COMMUNICATE

Invite children to present their work to the class and to challenge their classmates to guess the sorting rule.

ASSESSMENT OPPORTUNITY

The records that children create will show how well they can select and apply a sorting rule based on the type of energy. These recordings can be used as portfolio entries. LM B is provided to help you track portfolio entries. If children make presentations of their work, you can assess their ability to communicate their thinking orally. You can record your **observations** on AM 1.

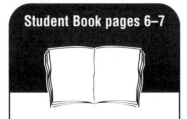

" How do wind-up toys work? "

PURPOSE:

– Describe how our senses of touch, hearing, and sight help us to control energy-using devices.

– Operate a simple device and identify the input and output.

– Ask questions about energy production.

– Plan investigations to answer some of these questions.

– Use appropriate vocabulary.

– Record relevant observations, findings, and measurements using written language, drawings, and charts.

– Communicate the procedures and results of investigations and explorations for specific purposes, using drawings and written descriptions.

MATERIALS:

• one small wind-up toy
• measuring tool
• LM 2 for each group

TIME:

1 class period

SKILL FOCUS

observing, comparing, inferring, experimenting

GET STARTED

Wind up a toy and let it go. Ask children to explain what you did and what happened as a result. Invite children to tell of other things that must be wound up to work, such as a music box or a clock.

Give small groups of children wind-up toys to explore. Call the groups together and have them tell about their wind-up toy. They can tell what it looks like, how it winds, and what it does. Ask:

■ What do you think makes the wind-up toy work?

Explain that when we wind something up, we are adding energy to it and that the item stores that energy. Releasing the stored energy makes the object work.

WORK ON IT

USING PAGES 6 AND 7

Explain that children will find out more about how a wind-up toy works by following the investigation outlined in the Student Book. Together, read through the instructions. Ensure that everyone understands the task.

Children might use such measuring tools as string, adding machine tape, or a cloth measuring tape. Make sure they understand how to use their measuring tool. Emphasize the importance of starting at the same place on the tool each time, and marking and recording the end point each time. If children are using adding

machine tape or string, they may wish to use cubes to determine the distance travelled for each trial in the experiment.

BEYOND THE PAGE

Provide small groups with a copy of LM 2. Explain that they can use it to record what they find out, and point out where they can record their first, second, and third trials. Make sure children understand that it is up to them to choose the number of times to wind the toy on the last trial.

Have children do the experiment and discuss their findings as they work. Encourage them to ask their own questions and make a plan for answering them. Ask:

■ What do you want to find out about these wind-up toys? What could you do to find that out?

Provide time for children to follow up on their ideas.

COMMUNICATE

When all the groups have finished the experiment, they can discuss their observations and recordings. Questions like these will promote discussion:

■ What did you find out? When did your toy move the farthest? How could we find out if all of the toys moved the same distance?

ASSESSMENT OPPORTUNITY

As you **observe** children at work you will be able to assess how comfortable they are operating a simple device and asking questions about how it works. **Observe** to see whether they approach the task in a reasonable sequence and whether they keep track of their findings. You can record your **observations** on AM 1. **Observations** you make of children at work might be recorded as anecdotes on AM 3.

" **Make a toy.** "

PURPOSE:

– Construct a manually controlled device that performs a specific task.

– Use appropriate vocabulary.

– Select one of the most common forms of energy used every day and predict the effect on their lives if it were no longer available.

MATERIALS:

• paper and drawing materials
• chart paper
• a variety of craft materials (heavy cardboard, pencil, bottle caps, small rubber balls, cardboard rolls, small boxes, empty spools, washers, small plastic yogurt containers, string, corks, lids, plastic fruit baskets, box of straws, pipe cleaners, toothpicks, popsicle sticks)

TIME:

2 to 3 class periods

SKILL FOCUS:

classifying, making models, communicating

GET STARTED

Invite pairs of children to draw pictures or print the name of their favourite toy. If the pairs cannot agree on one toy, they can record two. To initiate this you might say:

■ Imagine that someone wanted to buy a toy for someone your age. What toy would you suggest? Why?

Meet as a class and invite children to share their favourite toys. Record children's responses.

Create a second chart by grouping the toys on the first list according to how they work, but do not label the groups you create. Note that there may be toys suggested that work with electricity or batteries. Challenge children to identify your sorting rule. Ask:

■ How have I sorted the toys you suggested?

Give clues if needed. Continue this discussion of toys. Say:

■ You like these toys. Long ago there was no electricity. There were no batteries. Which of these toys would not have worked? Which of the toys on our chart do you think children played with long ago?

WORK ON IT

USING PAGES 8 AND 9

Encourage children to describe the toys they see on the page. Ask:

■ Have you ever seen toys like these? How are they all the same? How do you think they work? Would you like to play with any of them? Why?

Together read the directions for making a toy. Show children the materials you have collected and the working area. Ensure that everyone understands the task. Remind children that they can make any of the toys on the page or another toy.

BEYOND THE PAGE

As the children work, they may discover they need additional materials. Work together to collect those materials if possible.

When children are finished, encourage them to check their work to make sure the toy is finished to their satisfaction. Invite them to decorate their toy in any way they wish.

COMMUNICATE

Encourage children to share their toys with one another, and to describe the materials they used and any problems they encountered and tried to solve.

EXTENSION

Arrange a visit to a local pioneer village where children can gain further insight into how children of the past spent their time. Such a trip also engages children in thinking about how people lived without electricity.

ASSESSMENT OPPORTUNITY

Examining the children's toy creations gives you the opportunity to **observe** how children design and carry out plans. Observe who is willing to share ideas and help others and who has a creative streak. Note the children's ability to present orally. Since this toy is a significant piece of work you might consider taking a photo of it or asking children to draw a representation of it for inclusion in a **portfolio**. Use AM 1, AM 2, AM 3, and AM 4 for your recordings.

" Some toys use electricity and batteries. "

PURPOSE:

- Identify everyday uses of energy.
- Describe the different forms of energy used in a variety of everyday devices.
- Identify everyday devices that are controlled manually.

MATERIALS:

- chart paper
- magazines and catalogues for cutting up
- scissors
- glue
- paper

TIME:

2 class periods

SKILL FOCUS:

observing, classifying

GET STARTED

Flick the classroom lights on and off. Ask children to describe what you are doing (flicking the light switch). Ask:

- What happens when I flick the switch? (the lights go on or off)

Invite pairs or groups of children to brainstorm other things that they switch on and off. Have them write or draw their responses for later reference.
Meet as a large group. Ask:

- What items did you think of?

List the children's responses on chart paper. Explain that all of these things use electricity or batteries as a form of energy.

Things we switch
on and off

light switch
computer
TV
toy cars

WORK ON IT

USING PAGES 10 AND 11

Have children look at the toys on the page and describe them. Encourage children to tell which toys use electricity or run on batteries. Ask:

- How can you tell that a toy uses electricity? Batteries? What type of toys need this type of energy? What kind of toys need your energy? The energy of the wind?

Invite small groups of children to think of other electrical or battery-operated toys. Some children may prefer to work alone. Meet as a group to share ideas.

BEYOND THE PAGE

Provide small groups of children with magazines, flyers, and catalogues. Assign each group a type of energy that you have been discussing (batteries, electricity, human power, stored energy) or let groups choose one of their own. Have children go through the magazines and cut out pictures of items that use that particular form of energy. Children can draw or write the name of their type of energy on a large piece of paper, then create a collage by gluing down the pictures they find.

COMMUNICATE

Invite groups to share their collage with the class and to describe their form of energy and the objects that use it. Gather children's collages to create a class energy catalogue.

EXTENSION

Take the children to the school office. Encourage them to look for things that use different forms of energy. To initiate this you might ask:

- What uses electricity? Is there anything here that uses human energy? Gas? What form of energy do you think is used most?

ASSESSMENT OPPORTUNITY

As children work in small groups to create a recording you will have the chance to see how well they understand the different sources of energy. You can **observe** to see who is contributing ideas and listening to the ideas of others. AM 3 is a good place for you to note your **observations**.

> " Electricity makes lots of things work.
> Imagine a day without electricity. "

PURPOSE:

- Identify everyday uses of energy.
- Ask questions about needs and problems related to energy production or use in the immediate environment, and explore possible answers and solutions.
- Use appropriate vocabulary.
- Select one of the most common forms of energy used every day and predict the effect on their lives if it were no longer available.

MATERIALS:

- list of things that switch on and off from previous activity
- drawing materials
- LM 3 for each child

TIME:

2 class periods

SKILL FOCUS:

inferring, communicating

GET STARTED

Show children the chart they created in Activity 5 about things that turn on and off. Review with the children that all of those things use electricity or batteries. Encourage the children to point to the items on the list that they might find in school. Ask:

- Where in school would we find (a computer)?

Take the children on an electricity walk through the school, stopping to point out the items that they have listed. If possible, show them how each one turns on and off, and where the electricity source is (the source may be an electrical cord or a battery). Take notes as the children identify items. Back in class, add these items to the list.

WORK ON IT

USING PAGES 12 AND 13

Have children look at the picture on their own or with a partner and encourage them to draw or write a list of all the things in the picture that use electricity. Meet as a group to share what the children found. Create a comprehensive list on chart paper. Encourage children to add to the list by thinking of things in their own home that use electricity.

BEYOND THE PAGE

Engage children in thinking about what would happen in school if the electricity went out. Ask:

- Would we be able to see our work? (most likely natural sunlight would allow for this) Would we know what time it is? Would the bells work? Would the P.A. system work? What changes would we have to make?

Determine whether children have experienced power failures. Ask:

- Have you ever been someplace where the electricity has gone off? What did you do? What couldn't you do? Did you do anything special because of the power failure?

Invite children to use LM 3 to help them plan a day for their family without electricity. Remind children that they will need to see when it gets dark in the evening, and that they will need to prepare food and eat. Invite children to draw pictures to show how their family would adapt.

COMMUNICATE

Have children share and explain their completed plans in a large group.

ASSESSMENT OPPORTUNITY

The children's plans on LM 3 allow you to observe who understands how energy is used in daily life. Children's written records can become **portfolio** entries as they may reveal how well children can communicate ideas and organize thinking on paper. Track **portfolio** entries on AM 4.

SUSTAINABLE DEVELOPMENT

How would a day without electricity be better for our world?

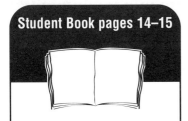

PURPOSE:

– Identify devices they use that consume energy and list things they can do to reduce energy consumption.

MATERIALS:

• Family Letter B (optional)

TIME:

1 to 2 class periods

SKILL FOCUS:

observing, inferring

At Home

GET STARTED

Ask:

- Are there times that we waste electricity in class?

They may notice that the lights are on even on sunny days, or that lights are not turned off when they leave the classroom for lunchtime.

Discuss with the children why it is important not to waste electricity. Explain that we use such things as coal, oil, and water to make electricity and that we do not want to run out of these very important resources.

WORK ON IT

USING PAGES 14 AND 15

Together review the pages. Remind children that they have already identified many places where electricity is used in school. Explain that they will now find places in their homes where electricity is used. Send home the Student Book or

Family Letter B for children and their families to complete the activity together. If you choose to do the activity in the classroom, children can refocus on the places they saw electricity in use at school, then make posters to help remind them to conserve energy.

COMMUNICATE

After children have learned more about the electrical devices in their homes and have discussed with family members how to reduce their use, have a group discussion. You might ask questions like these to promote discussion:

- What things did you find that use electricity? Which of these do you use a lot? How could you use them less? Describe the posters and signs you made. What did they look like? What did you write on them? Where did you decide to hang the posters? Do you think that you are starting to use less electricity?

PURPOSE:

– Describe the different forms of energy used in a variety of everyday devices.

SKILL FOCUS:

observing

Look Back

WORK ON IT

USING PAGE 16

Together, read page 16 in the Student Book. Ask the children to describe each part of the machine and how each works together to make the machine work. Then have children complete the activity on the page by finding each item from the machine somewhere in the book.

ANSWERS

The machine works as follows:
The clock strikes 5 (electrical energy), lifting the blocks from under the truck's wheels. The truck moves down the ramp (movement energy), opening the fridge door. The balls fall out of the fridge (movement energy) onto the platform with the finger. The finger pushes the button to start the train moving (electrical energy). The train whistle (sound energy)

scares the cat, which leaps from the plank (movement energy), tipping the cereal into the bowl.

The clock is on page 12, the blocks are on page 11, the truck is on page 11, the fridge is on page 12, 14, and 15, the ball is on page 5, the train is on page 10, the cat is on page 12, and the rooster is on page 2.

COMMUNICATE

Invite children to share what they found, and to talk about what they learned about energy in the world around them.

ASSESSMENT OPPORTUNITY

Provide children with a copy of AM 5 for self-assessment. Discuss children's answers with them individually, and store completed Assessment Masters in children's portfolios.

Demonstrate What You Know

PURPOSE:

– Assess children's learning.

MATERIALS:

- energy web from Keep It Going
- LM 4 for each child
- drawing and writing materials

SKILL FOCUS:

communicating, classifying, inferring

GET STARTED

Draw children's attention to the web that you began during the unit launch. Ask:

- Are there any other words that we can add to our Energy web?

Add any words children suggest, prompting them by recalling activities they have done during the unit. Extend the web by choosing one of the words on it and making a web for that word (for example, a web for sun could include the words food, animals, plants; a web for electricity could include the words water, oil, refrigerator).

ASSIGN THE TASK

Provide each child with LM 4. You can do this assessment task individually, in small groups, or as a whole class. Have the children circle the toys, on the top part of the page, that use electricity. Then challenge them to think of other things that use electricity. Encourage them to

think of things in the classroom, at home, around the school, or in other places. Have children draw their items in place on the web at the bottom of the page.

Have children tell about the items that they drew on their web. Choose one item (for example, a light) and say:

- What do you need light for? (to read) How else could you read if there were no lights? (use sunlight,use a candle, use a battery-operated flashlight, use light from acampfire).

Ask children to choose one of the items they drew on the web and challenge them to think of what they would have to do if the electricity went off and they could not use the item. Children can draw their response on the back of LM 4.

ASSESS THE TASK

The following rubric will help you assess each child's learning about energy.

Performance Task Rubric	
Rubric	**Criteria**
Level 4	• child identifies all toys that use electricity • child draws 3 or more items on the web • child has a clear, more complex solution for the problem of having no electricity
Level 3	• child identifies most toys that use electricity • child draws at least 2 items on the web • child has a clear solution for the problem of having no electricity
Level 2	• child identifies 1 toy that use electricity • child draws at least 1 item on the web • child requires a lot of assistance to solve the problem of having no electricity
Level I	• child cannot identify the toys that use electricity • child draws no items on the web • child cannot solve the problem of having no electricity

Family Letter Ⓐ

Dear Family,

We will be investigating toys as part of a science unit called Energy for Work and Play. We will look at different forms of energy that power toys and other common devices.

Here are some activities that you can do at home to extend and reinforce our science curriculum. I hope that you enjoy them!

▶ Ask your child to tell you about the electricity-free day he or she planned at school. Together, try some of the ideas.

▶ The sun is the principal source of energy used on Earth. Your child has discussed how heat and light from the sun give plants their energy. To help make this point more concretely, place a small plant on a window ledge and another in a spot away from natural sunlight. Water both on the same schedule. Encourage your child to make observations over time. Together talk about how the plants compare.

▶ We use our senses to decide when to control energy. Try to point out examples — you hear the alarm on the clock and know to turn it off, you feel the bath water and know to adjust the temperature, you smell something burning and know to reduce the heat.

▶ Food is our source of energy. To help children make this connection try to connect food to their activity. Saying things such as the following can help make such connections: "You need to eat something or you'll have no energy." "You just played outdoors for a long time. You must be thirsty and hungry after using so much of your energy."

✂ -

ENERGY FOR WORK AND PLAY

Family Letter Ⓑ

Dear Family,

We have begun discussing the following activity in the classroom, and hope you will enjoy completing the activity with your child.

With your child, walk through your home. Have your child tell you all the places that electricity is used. Together, discuss ways to conserve energy by using less electricity. Invite your child to make posters that remind family members how they can help conserve energy.

 Copyright © 2000 Pearson Education Canada Inc.

Toys

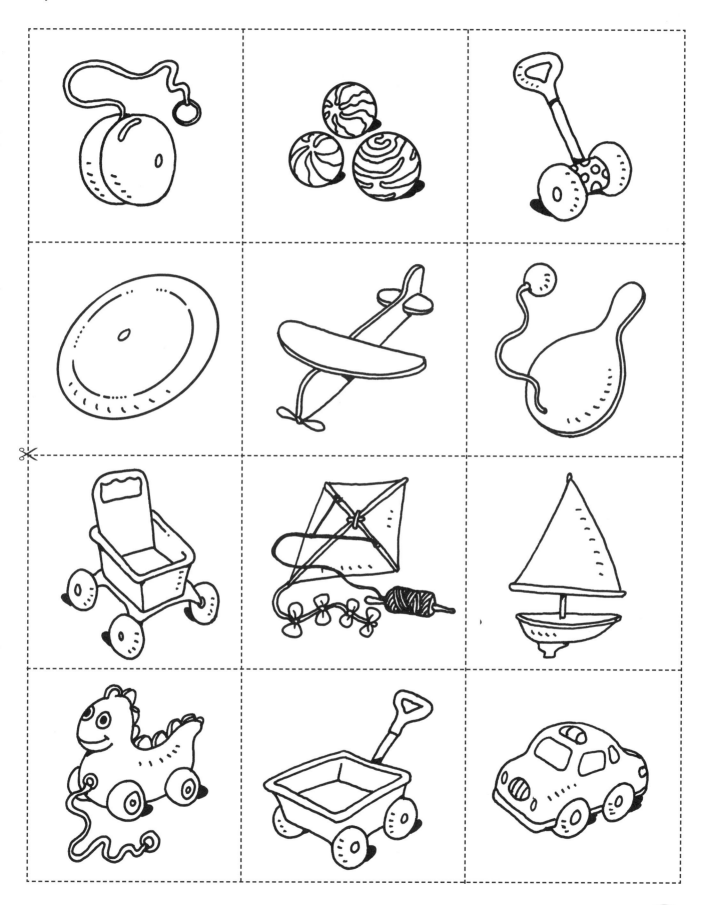

Name: _____   Date: _____

Test a Toy

Draw your wind-up toy.

	How many times did you wind it?	**How far does it travel?**
First time	_____	_____
Second time	_____	_____
Third time	_____	_____

    Copyright © 2000 Pearson Education Canada Inc.

Name: _____   Date: _____

A Day with No Electricity

Things that use electricity

We could play	We could eat
We could see by	**We could keep warm by**

Copyright © 2000 Pearson Education Canada Inc.   Energy for Work and Play

Name: _____   Date: _____

Circle the toys that use electricity.

On the web, draw other things that use electricity.

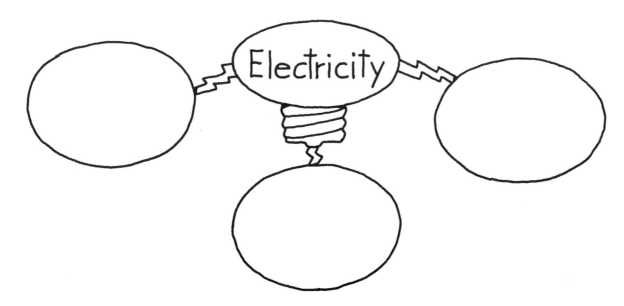

Electricity

What could you use if there were no electricity?
Turn the page and draw.

Energy for Work and Play   Copyright © 2000 Pearson Education Canada Inc.